Creative Publications

Grades 1–10

Tangramath

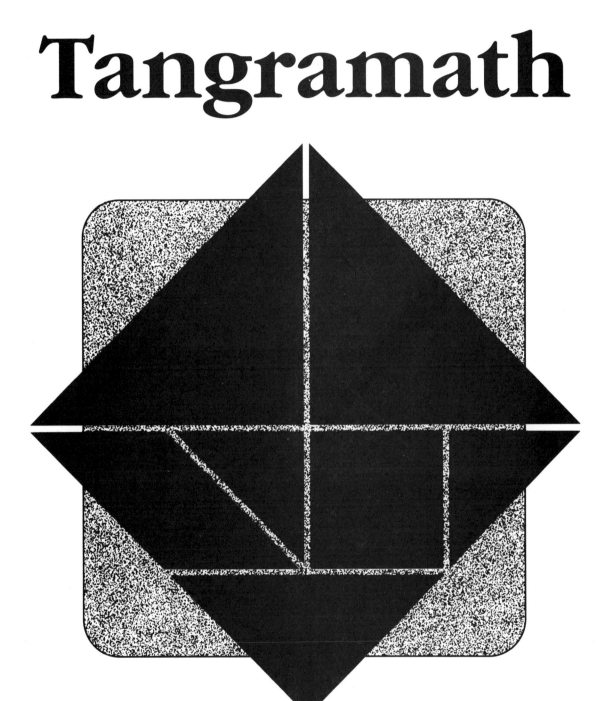

Dale Seymour

TANGRAMATH

Creative Publications is a registered trademark.

Cartoons by Bob Larsen
Tangram Drawings by William T. Stokes

©1971 Creative Publications
Two Prudential Plaza, Suite 1175
Chicago, IL 60601
Printed in U.S.A.

ISBN: 0-88488-148-2

22232425.0302010099

INTRODUCTION

The seven—piece tangram puzzle originated in China where it enjoyed a great deal of popularity in the early 1800's.

The puzzle involved manipulating a square, a parallelogram and five triangles into silhouette patterns of people, animals, objects or geometric figures. Construction of the seven tangram pieces varied from elaborately carved ivory to wooden or cardboard sets. The origin of the puzzle and its name are open to speculation. In 1903 Sam Loyd, the famous puzzle expert, published a book of tangram patterns along with a detailed account of the origin of the puzzle. As one might suspect from a master puzzle buff, Loyd's history of the tangram turned out to be a well—planned spoof.

Due to the recent emphasis on learning concepts of mathematics through the use of manipulative materials coupled with the natural fascination of puzzles, it is no surprise that the tangram puzzle has become a popular teaching device in the classroom. Many aspects of these shapes lend themselves to the discovery or discussion of concepts such as size, shape, congruence, similarity, properties of polygons, symmetry and area.

This book was designed for use by a wide range of age and ability levels. It may serve as a workbook by itself to be used by one student proceeding at his own rate in an individualized setting, or a teacher may wish to extract certain sections of the book to duplicate for use with an entire class. If two books are purchased, a set of "activity" or "task" cards could be made — with the teacher or student pasting the pages to sturdier cardboard sheets and then laminating them for protection.

The activities in this book are only some examples of the variety of ways in which tangram shapes can be used to reinforce mathematical concepts. Suggested open—ended activities are listed at the end of each of the three sections in the book. The sizes of the tangram pieces lend themselves well to use on the overhead projector. Overhead transparencies of selected pages can be made by use of the school's reproduction facilities.

Sets of tangram pieces can be made by students or teachers from colored paper or cardboard. Commercial sets in wood or plastic are inexpensive.

HAVE FUN WITH TANGRAMS!

PART ONE

THE TANGRAM SHAPES

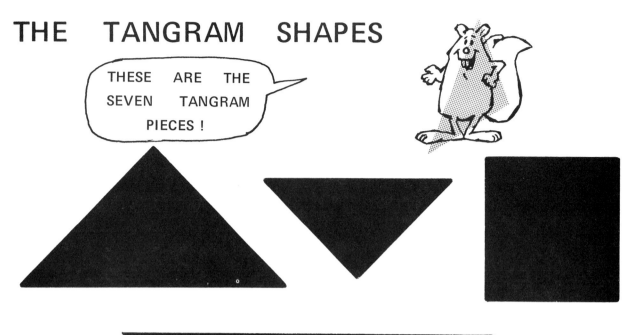

THESE ARE THE SEVEN TANGRAM PIECES !

PLACE YOUR TANGRAM PIECES ON THE SHAPES ABOVE.

(IF YOU DON'T HAVE A SET OF TANGRAM SHAPES, YOU MAY WANT TO MAKE YOUR OWN FROM THE PATTERNS ABOVE.)

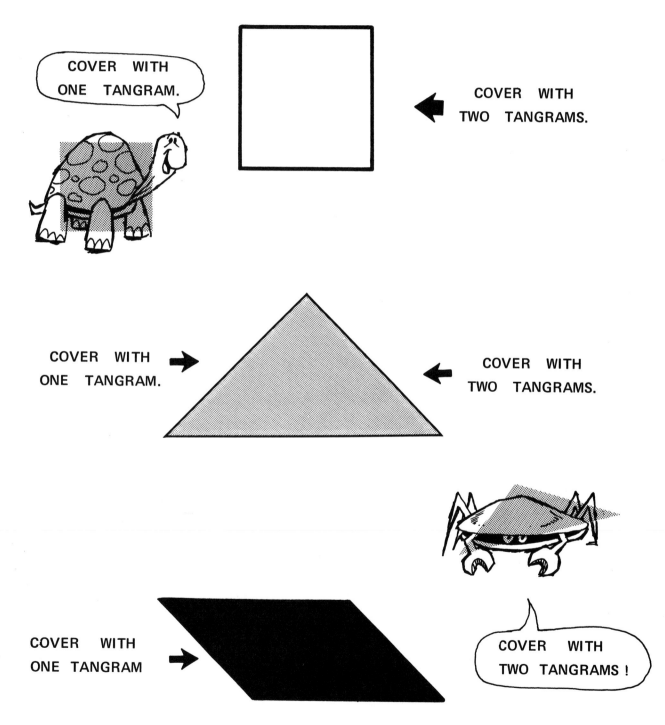

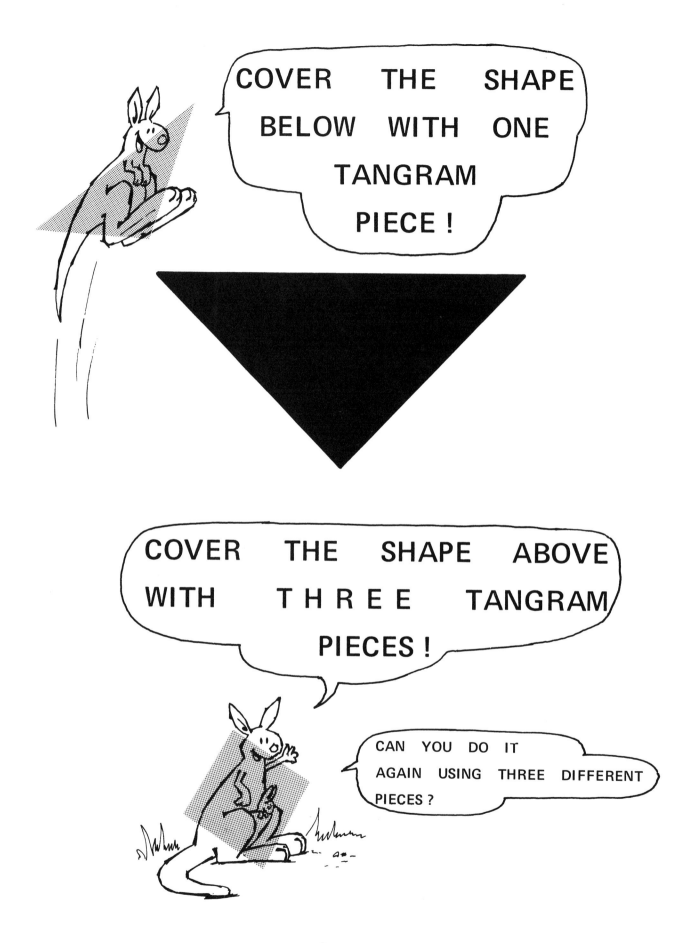

THE TANGRAM PIECES

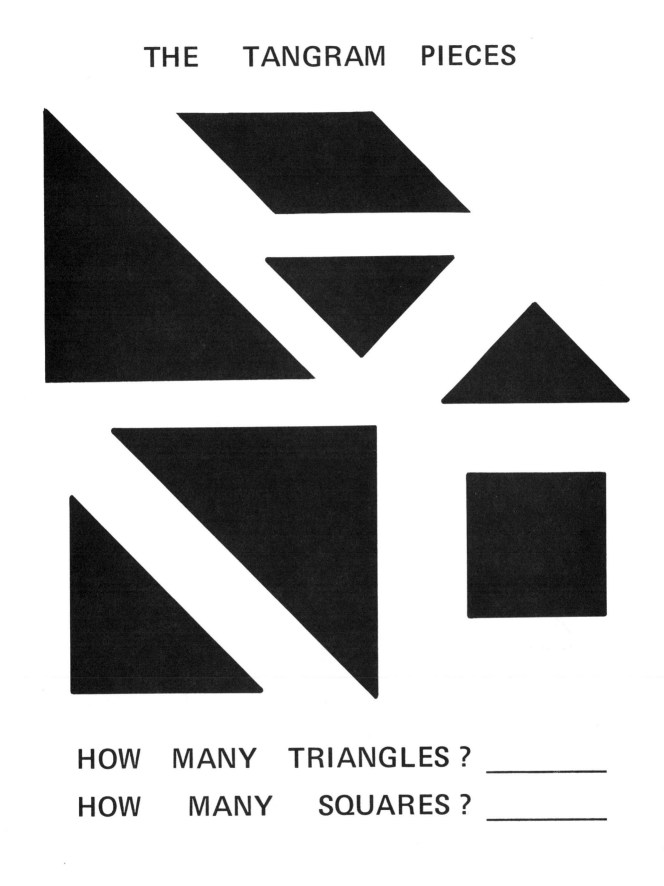

HOW   MANY   TRIANGLES ? _____

HOW   MANY   SQUARES ? _____

FIT THE TANGRAM SHAPES !

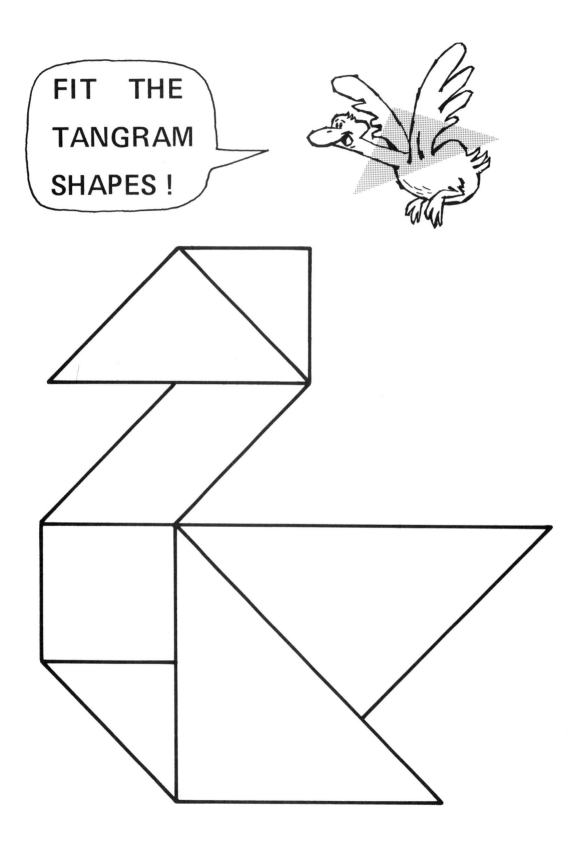

13

YOU WILL NEED TO "FLIP" THE
PARALLELOGRAM PIECE TO HAVE IT
FIT OVER BOTH SHAPES BELOW.

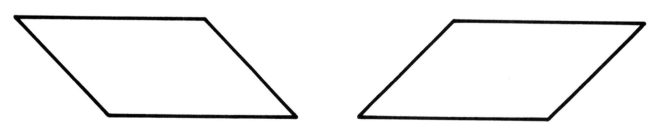

IN THIS BOOK IT IS ALRIGHT TO TURN
OVER OR "FLIP" A TANGRAM PIECE
WHEN YOU ARE WORKING A PUZZLE.

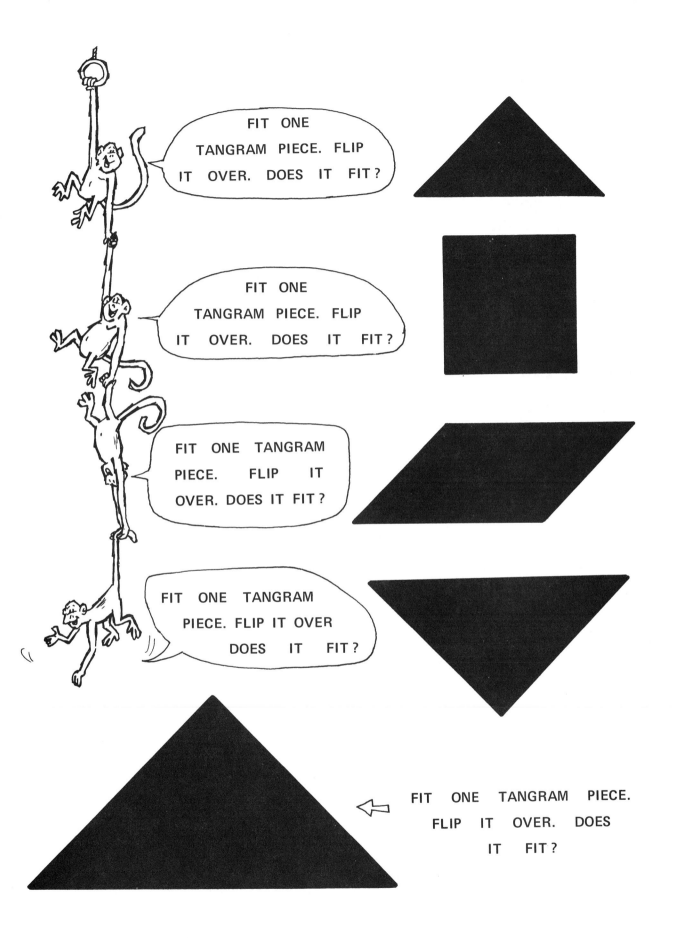

DID YOU NEED TO TURN
THE PARALLELOGRAM OVER
TO FIT THE SHAPES ABOVE?

REMEMBER! IN MANY PUZZLES WHICH USE THE
PARALLELOGRAM TANGRAM PIECE, IT MAY BE
NECESSARY TO FLIP THE PIECE OVER.

TANGRAMATH ©1971 Creative Publications

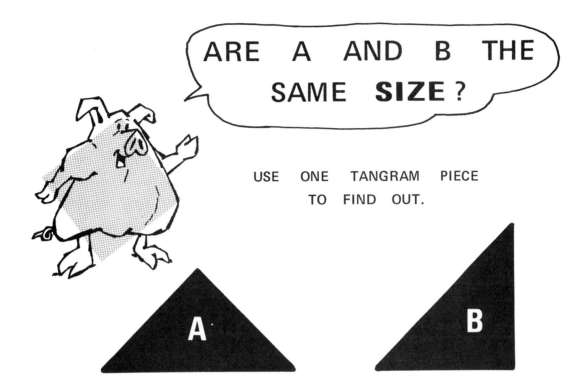

ARE A AND B THE SAME **SIZE**?

USE ONE TANGRAM PIECE TO FIND OUT.

ARE C AND D THE SAME **SIZE**?

USE THE TWO SMALL TRIANGLES TO HELP ANSWER THIS QUESTION.

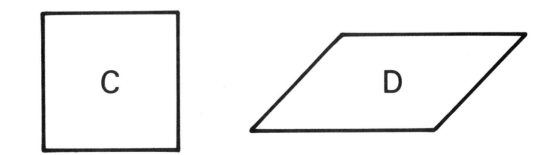

FIT THE TANGRAM SHAPES!

WHAT OTHER LETTERS OF THE ALPHABET CAN YOU MAKE USING ALL SEVEN TANGRAM PIECES?

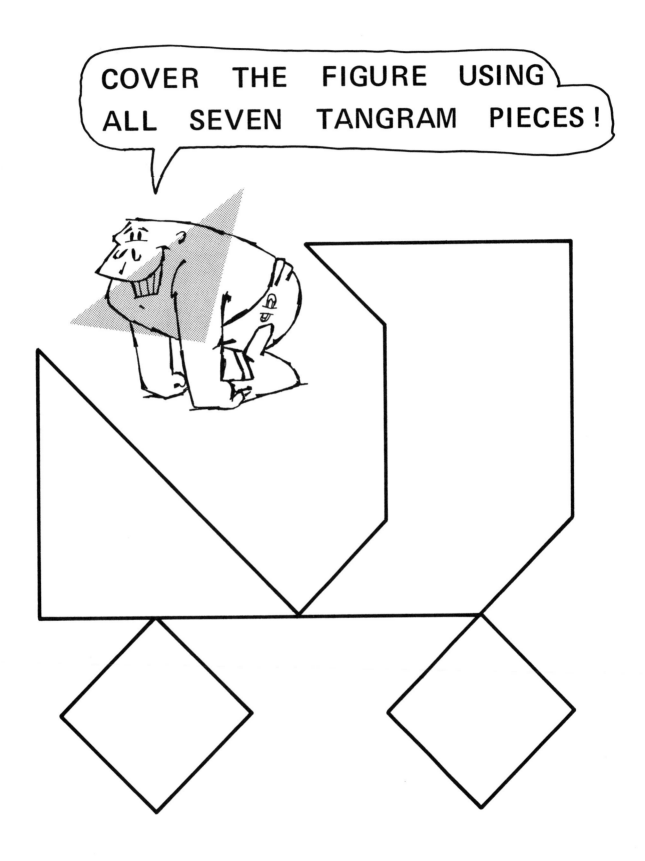

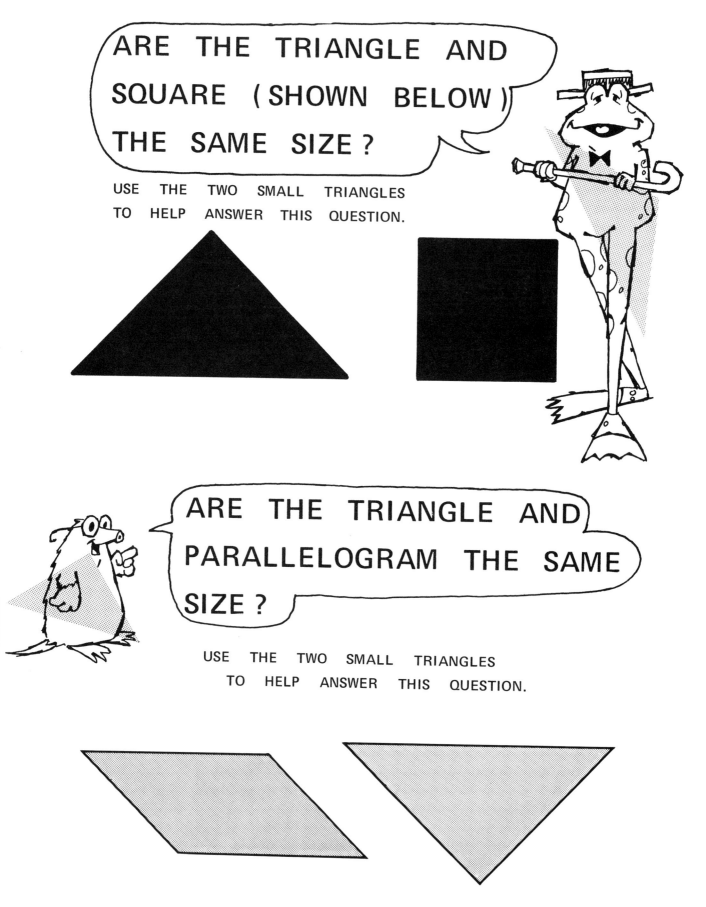

ARE THE TRIANGLE AND SQUARE (SHOWN BELOW) THE SAME SIZE?

USE THE TWO SMALL TRIANGLES TO HELP ANSWER THIS QUESTION.

ARE THE TRIANGLE AND PARALLELOGRAM THE SAME SIZE?

USE THE TWO SMALL TRIANGLES TO HELP ANSWER THIS QUESTION.

FIGURES 1, 2, AND 3 ARE
ALL THE SAME _____.

EACH OF THE FIGURES ABOVE
CAN BE COVERED EXACTLY BY
THE TWO SMALL TRIANGLES.
TRY IT!

FIGURES CAN BE THE SAME SIZE
AND NOT HAVE THE SAME SHAPE!

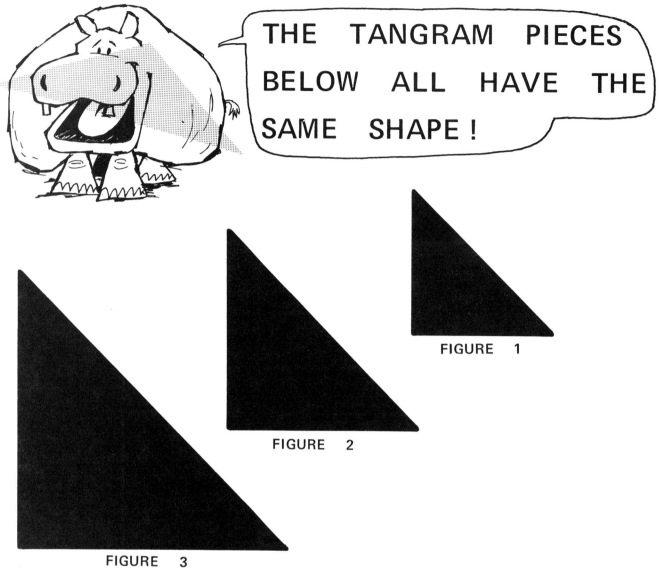

THE TANGRAM PIECES BELOW ALL HAVE THE SAME SHAPE !

FIGURE 1

FIGURE 2

FIGURE 3

THESE TANGRAM PIECES ARE NOT ALL THE SAME SIZE.

HOW MANY OF THE SMALL TANGRAM TRIANGLES FIT INTO FIGURE 1? _____

HOW MANY FIT INTO FIGURE 2? _____

HOW MANY FIT INTO FIGURE 3? _____

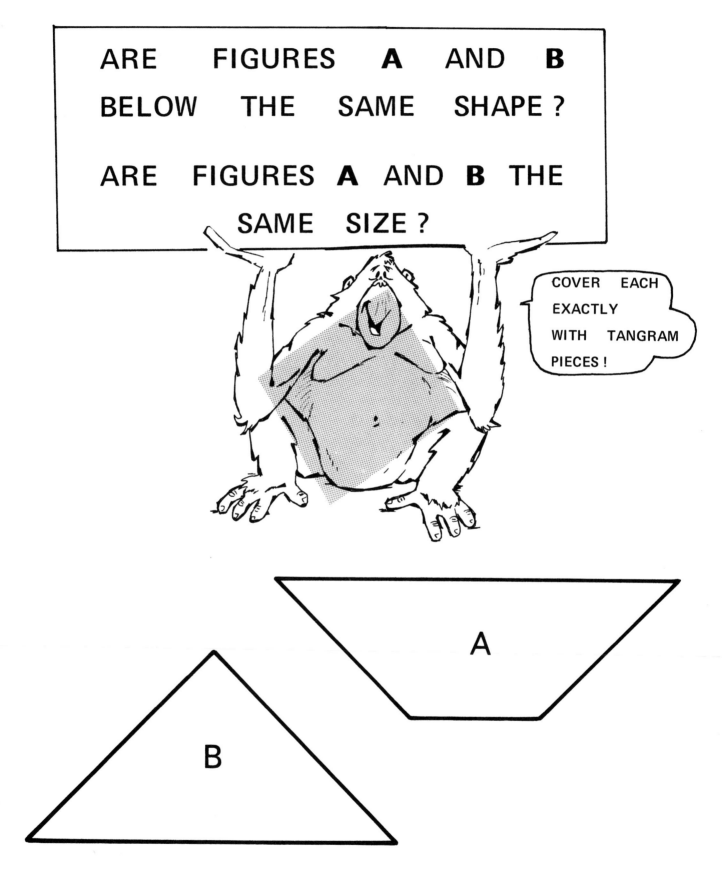

ARE FIGURES **A** AND **B** BELOW THE SAME SHAPE ?

ARE FIGURES **A** AND **B** THE SAME SIZE ?

COVER EACH EXACTLY WITH TANGRAM PIECES !

A

B

23

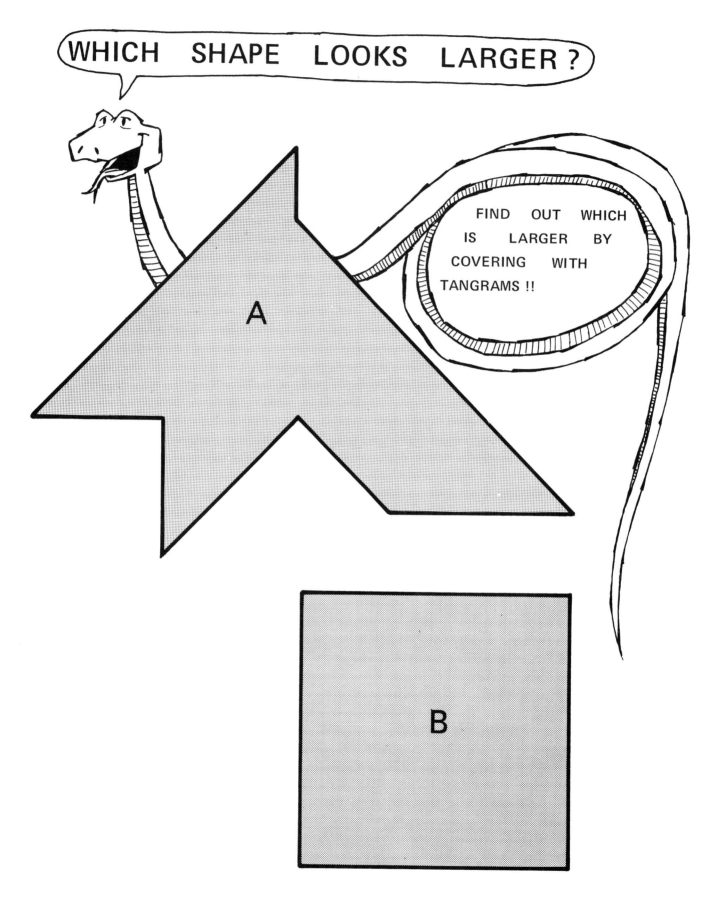

24

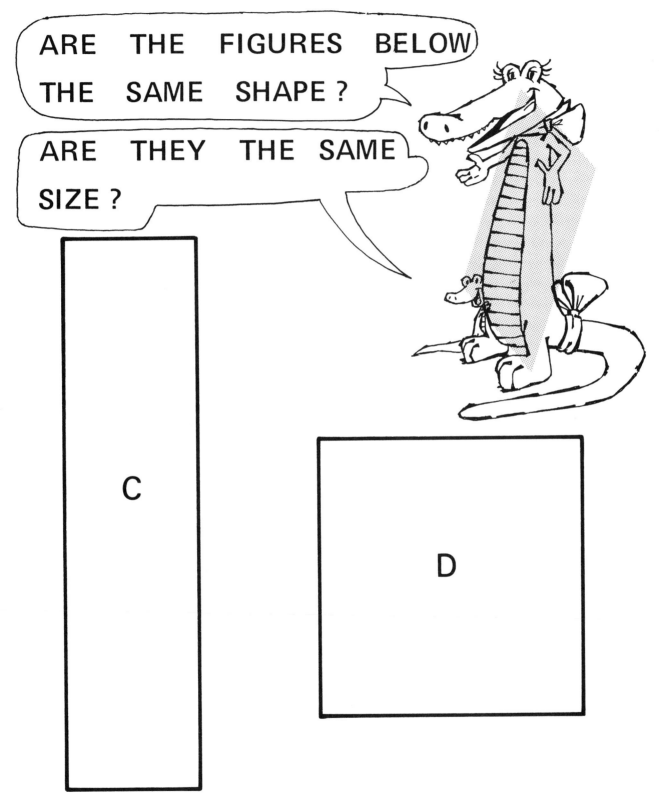

ARE THE FIGURES BELOW THE SAME SHAPE?

ARE THEY THE SAME SIZE?

C

D

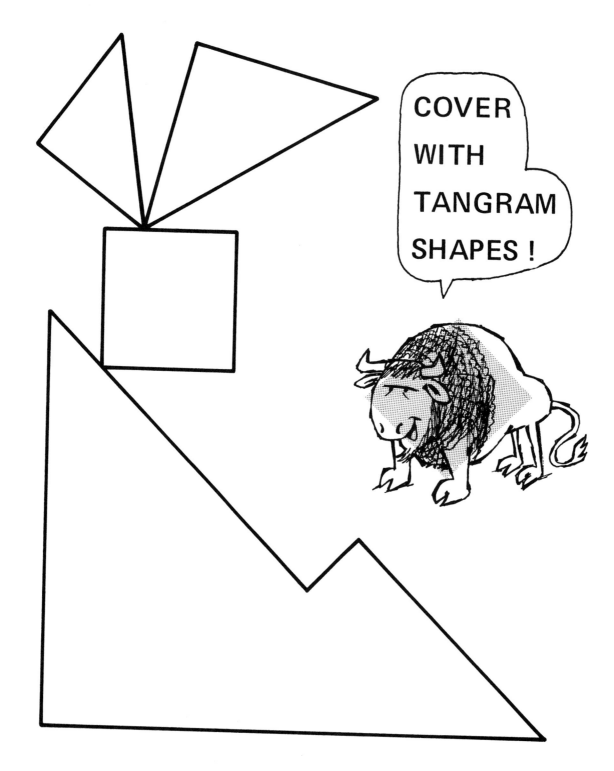

COVER WITH TANGRAM SHAPES !

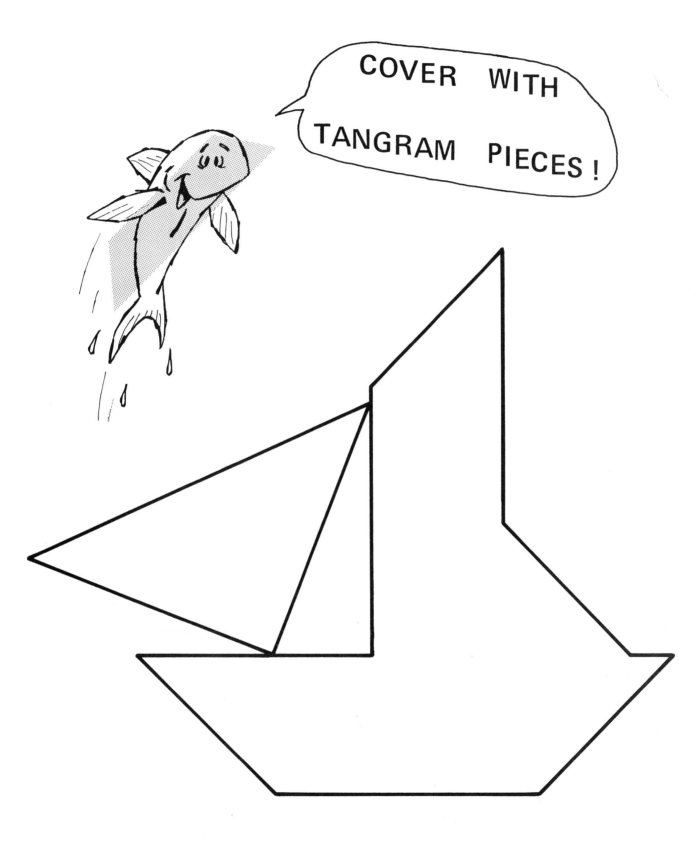

29

SUGGESTED ACTIVITIES

PART 1

1) Create some of your own patterns using the tangram pieces. (People, animals, birds, fish, boats, geometric designs, etc.)

2) Make a puzzle. Trace its outline. Give it to a friend to "solve".

3) How many <u>different</u> ways can you form square B on Page 24.

4) Cut some tangrams from colored paper and design a creative bulletin board display of tangram patterns.

5) Design a difficult tangram puzzle for your principal to solve.

PART TWO

THE SEVEN SHAPES BELOW ARE THE SEVEN TANGRAM PIECES. THE TANGRAM PUZZLE ORIGINATED IN CHINA. HUNDREDS OF PUZZLES CAN BE MADE USING THE TANGRAMS. TAN—GRAMS CAN ALSO BE USED TO MAKE LEARNING MATHEMATICS MORE INTERESTING. IF YOU DON'T HAVE A SET OF TANGRAMS YOU MAY USE THESE SHAPES AS A PATTERN.

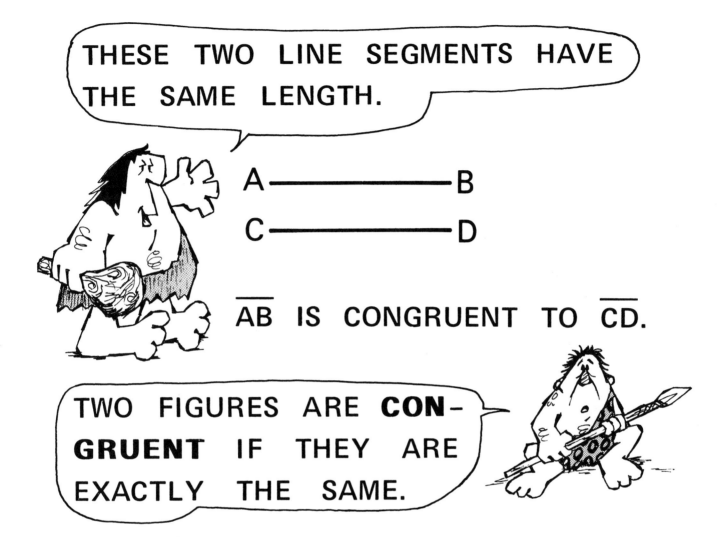

THESE TWO LINE SEGMENTS HAVE THE SAME LENGTH.

A ——————— B
C ——————— D

$\overline{AB}$ IS CONGRUENT TO $\overline{CD}$.

TWO FIGURES ARE **CONGRUENT** IF THEY ARE EXACTLY THE SAME.

FIT A SMALL TANGRAM TRIANGLE IN THE FIGURE BELOW.

FLIP IT OVER AND FIT IT AGAIN.

NOW ANSWER THESE QUESTIONS:

    IS $\overline{AB}$ CONGRUENT TO $\overline{AC}$? _____

    IS $\overline{AB}$ CONGRUENT TO $\overline{BC}$? _____

COVER THE TWO SHAPES BELOW WITH THE SMALL TRIANGLES!

SLIDE THEM TO THE CENTER UNTIL THEY MEET TO MAKE A LARGE TRIANGLE.

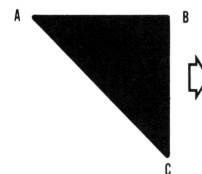

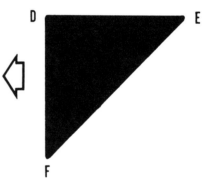

IS $\overline{BC}$ CONGRUENT TO $\overline{DF}$? ___

FIT ONE SMALL TRIANGLE EXACTLY ON THE OTHER. THESE TWO FIGURES ARE SAID TO BE **CONGRUENT** BECAUSE THEY ARE THE SAME IN EVERY WAY.

USE THE TANGRAM PIECES THAT ARE CONGRUENT TO TO THE THREE SHAPES BELOW TO ANSWER THE QUESTIONS !

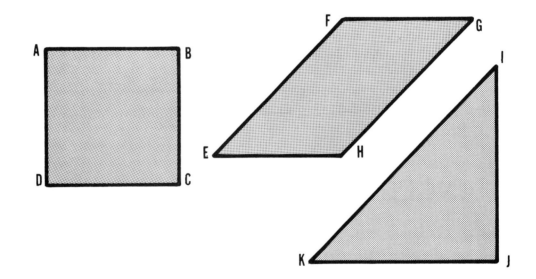

WHICH SIDES OF THE PARALLELOGRAM (IF ANY) ARE CONGRUENT TO THE SIDES OF THE SQUARE?

_____

WHICH SIDES OF THE TRIANGLE (IF ANY) ARE CON-GRUENT TO WHICH SIDES OF THE PARALLELOGRAM?

_____

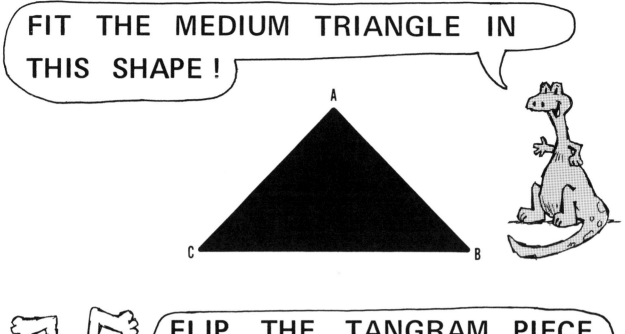

FIT THE MEDIUM TRIANGLE IN THIS SHAPE!

FLIP THE TANGRAM PIECE OVER...FIT IN THE SHAPE AGAIN!

IS ANGLE **B** CONGRUENT TO ANGLE **C**?

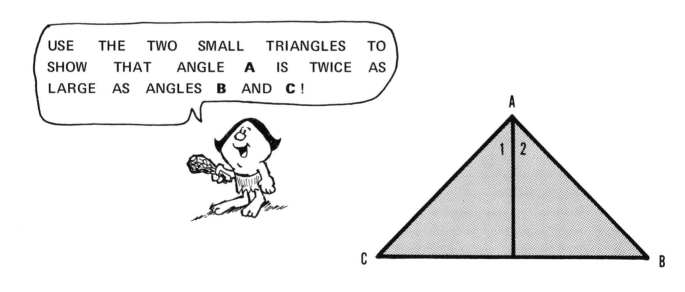

USE THE TWO SMALL TRIANGLES TO SHOW THAT ANGLE **A** IS TWICE AS LARGE AS ANGLES **B** AND **C**!

IS ANGLE 1 CONGRUENT TO ANGLE C?

36

USE ALL SEVEN TANGRAMS TO FORM THE FIGURE BELOW!

USE ALL THE SEVEN TANGRAMS TO FORM THE FIGURE BELOW!

A TRIANGLE WITH TWO SIDES CONGRUENT IS **ISOSCELES**!

CAN YOU "FLIP" YOUR TANGRAM PIECES TO PROVE THAT THE TRIANGLES BELOW ARE ISOSCELES TRIANGLES ?

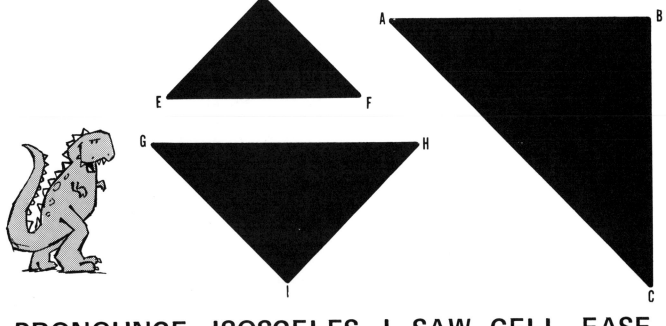

PRONOUNCE ISOSCELES I–SAW–CELL–EASE.

THE FOUR "SQUARE CORNERS" OF A SQUARE ARE CALLED **RIGHT ANGLES**!

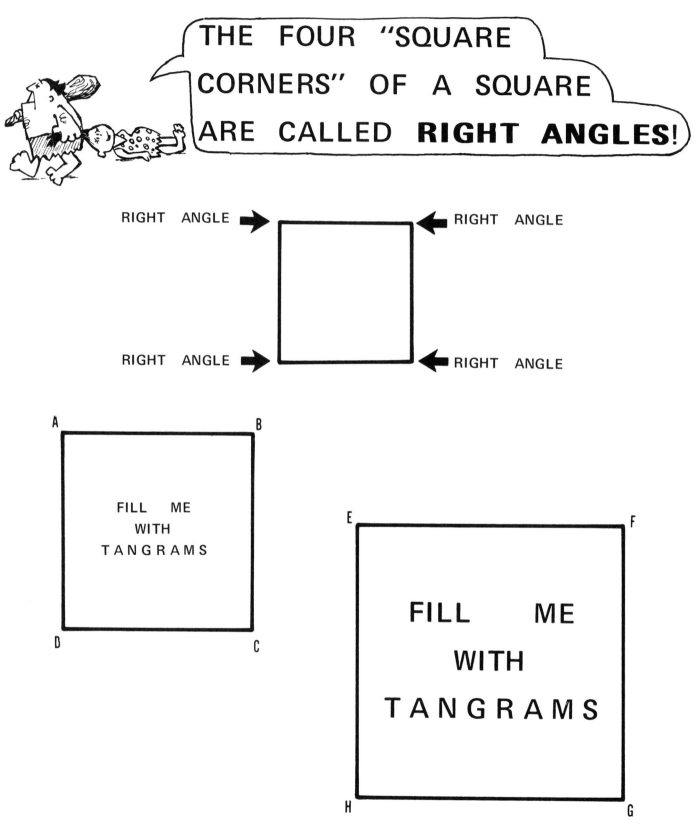

RIGHT ANGLE ➡   ⬅ RIGHT ANGLE

RIGHT ANGLE ➡   ⬅ RIGHT ANGLE

A   B

FILL   ME
WITH
TANGRAMS

D   C

E   F

FILL   ME

WITH

TANGRAMS

H   G

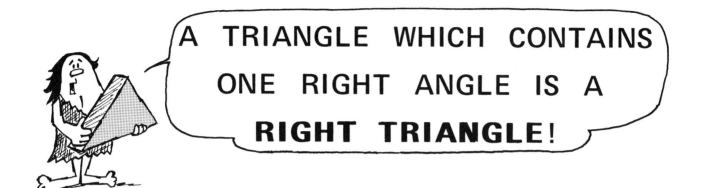

A TRIANGLE WHICH CONTAINS ONE RIGHT ANGLE IS A **RIGHT TRIANGLE**!

USE YOUR TANGRAM SQUARE TO SHOW THAT EACH OF THE THREE TRIANGLES BELOW CONTAINS ONE RIGHT ANGLE.

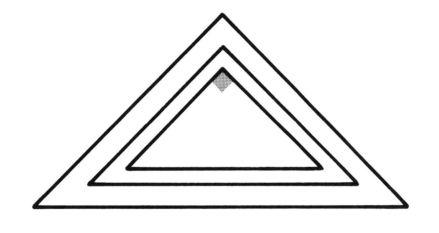

DO ALL FIVE OF THE TANGRAM TRIANGLES CONTAIN ONE RIGHT ANGLE?

ARE ALL FIVE OF THE TANGRAM TRIANGLES RIGHT TRIANGLES?

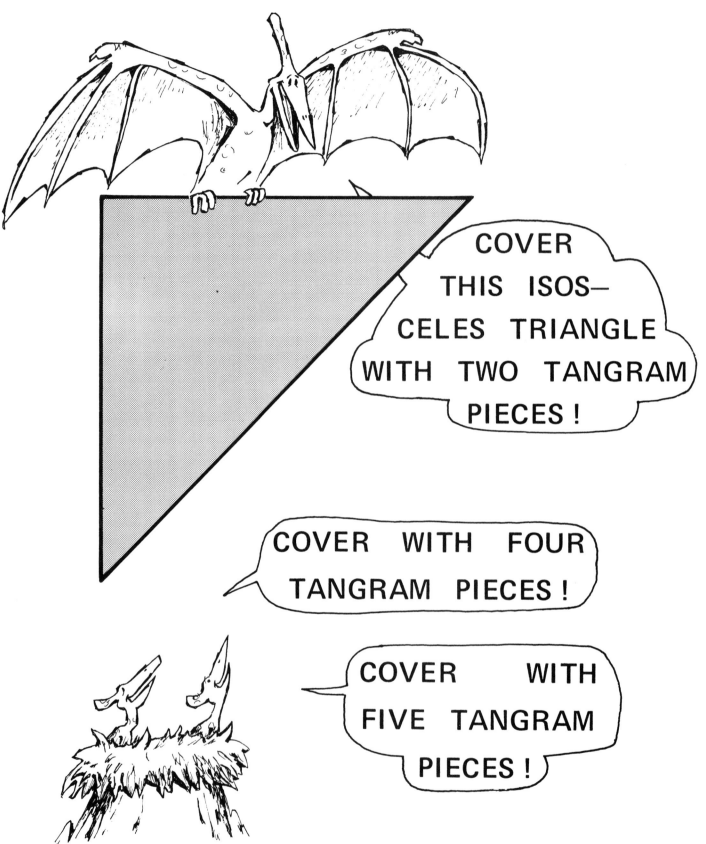

COVER THIS ISOS— CELES TRIANGLE WITH TWO TANGRAM PIECES !

COVER WITH FOUR TANGRAM PIECES !

COVER WITH FIVE TANGRAM PIECES !

COVER
WITH TANGRAMS

COVER WITH TANGRAMS

1. COVER THIS SQUARE WITH THE TANGRAM SQUARE PIECE!

2. THEN TURN THE TANGRAM 1/4 OF A COMPLETE TURN.

3. TURN IT 1/4 AGAIN.

4. TURN IT 1/4 ONCE MORE.

DOES THE TANGRAM PIECE COVER THE SHAPE ALL FOUR WAYS? _____

DOES THIS SHOW THAT THE FOUR SIDES ARE CONGRUENT? _____

ARE ALL FOUR ANGLES CONGRUENT? _____

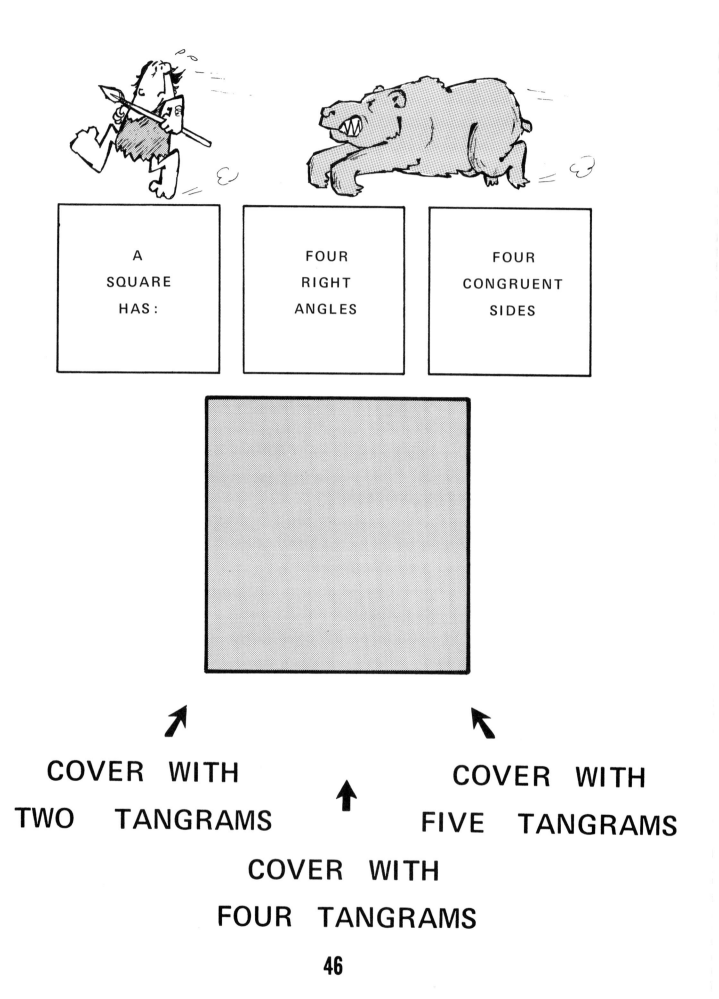

A SQUARE HAS:

FOUR RIGHT ANGLES

FOUR CONGRUENT SIDES

COVER WITH TWO TANGRAMS

COVER WITH FOUR TANGRAMS

COVER WITH FIVE TANGRAMS

USE ALL SEVEN TANGRAMS TO FORM THE FIGURE BELOW!

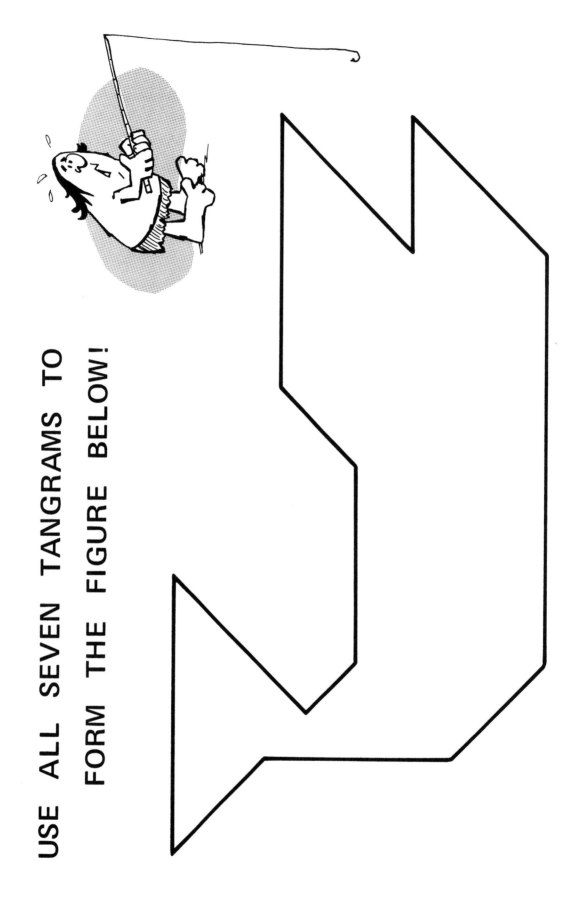

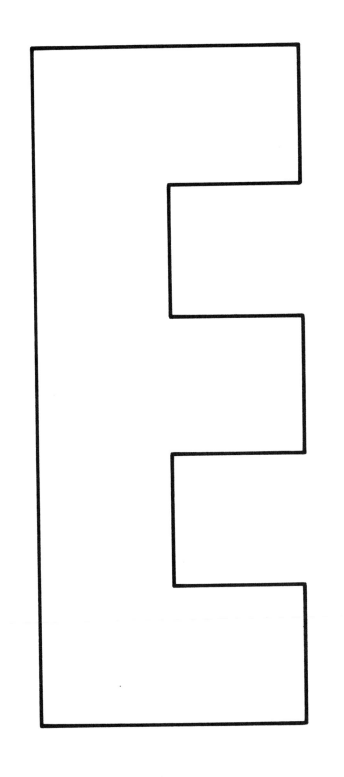

USE ALL SEVEN TANGRAMS TO FORM THE FIGURE AT THE LEFT.

THE **PARALLELOGRAM** GETS ITS NAME FROM THE FACT THAT ITS OPPOSITE SIDES ARE PARALLEL.

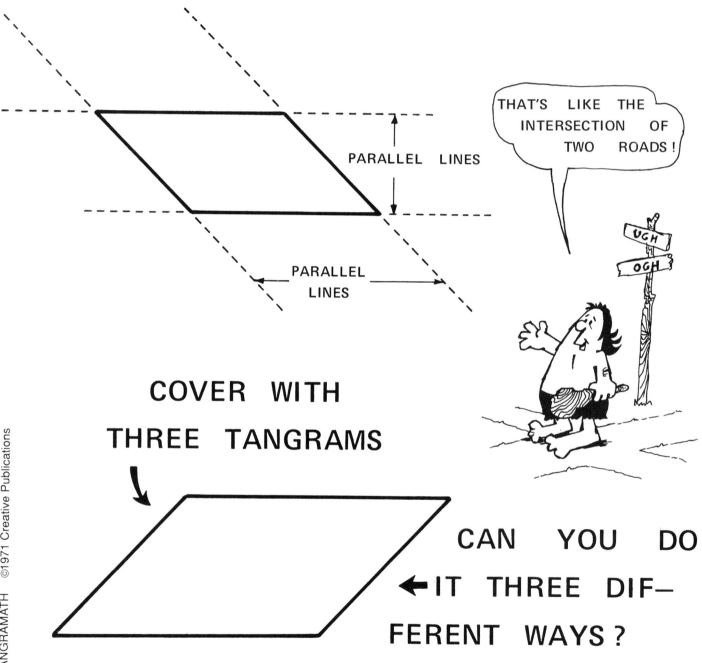

PARALLEL LINES

PARALLEL LINES

THAT'S LIKE THE INTERSECTION OF TWO ROADS!

UGH

OGH

COVER WITH THREE TANGRAMS

CAN YOU DO IT THREE DIF- FERENT WAYS?

USE THE MEDIUM TRIANGLE TAN—GRAM TO "MEASURE" AND VERIFY THE PROPERTIES STATED BELOW!

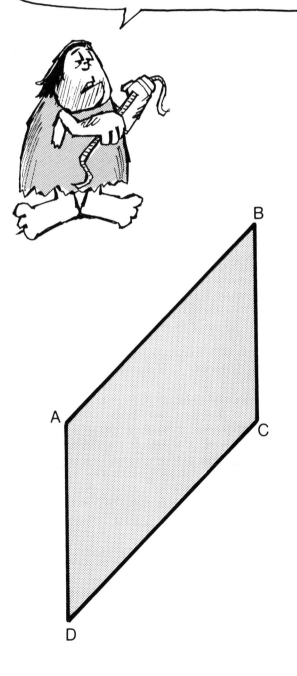

THE OPPOSITE SIDES OF A **PARALLELOGRAM** ARE CONGRUENT.

THE OPPOSITE ANGLES OF A **PARALLELOGRAM** ARE CONGRUENT.

COVER
WITH
TAN—
GRAM
PIECES.

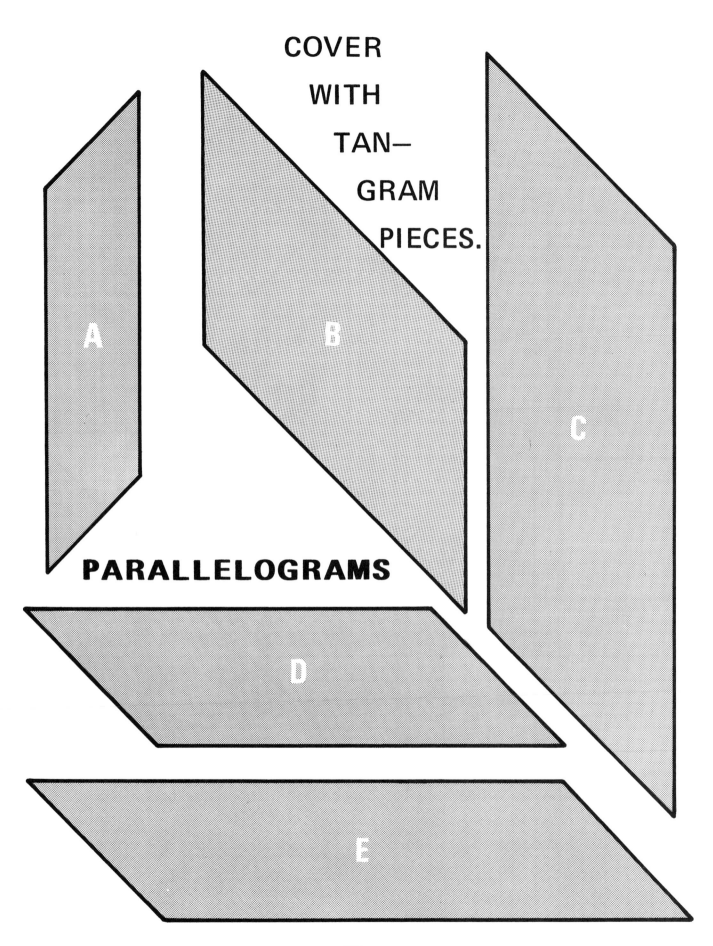

PARALLELOGRAMS

TANGRAMATH

THE   DOTTED
LINES ON THIS
PAGE   ARE
DIAGONALS.

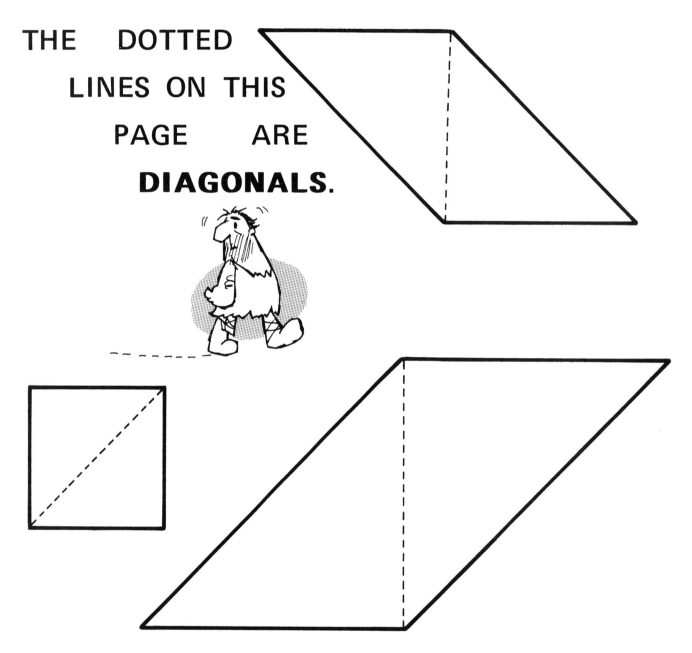

USE   TANGRAM   PIECES   TO   SHOW   THAT   THE   DIAGONALS   DIVIDE   THESE
PARALLELOGRAMS   INTO   TWO   CONGRUENT   SHAPES.

TANGRAMATH   ©1971 Creative Publications

A RECTANGLE IS A SPECIAL PARALLELOGRAM. IT HAS FOUR RIGHT ANGLES.

COVER THE RECTANGLES BELOW WITH TANGRAM PIECES!

HOW MANY DIFFERENT WAYS CAN YOU COVER THE LONGER RECTANGLE?

ARE THE OPPOSITE SIDES OF A RECTANGLE CONGRUENT?

ARE THE OPPOSITE ANGLES OF A RECTANGLE CONGRUENT?

ARE THE OPPOSITE SIDES OF A RECTANGLE PARALLEL?

COVER THE RECTANGLE WITH TANGRAMS

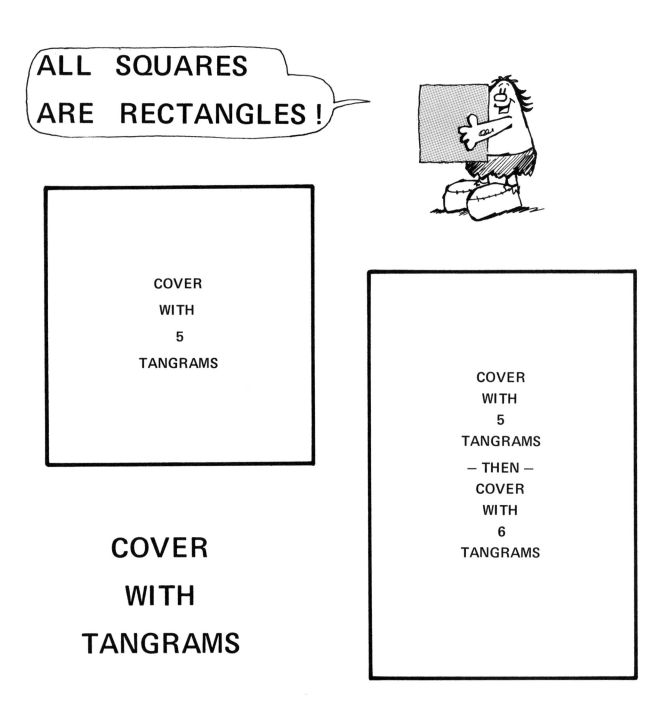

ALL SQUARES
ARE RECTANGLES!

COVER
WITH
5
TANGRAMS

COVER
WITH
5
TANGRAMS
— THEN —
COVER
WITH
6
TANGRAMS

COVER

WITH

TANGRAMS

SUGGESTED ACTIVITIES

PART 2

1) Use the tangram pieces to form each letter of the alphabet. Trace your patterns.

2) Use the tangram pieces to form the numerals 0, 1, 2, 3, 4, 5, 6, 7, 8, 9. (Some of them may be pretty "weird".)

3) What tangram pieces are symmetrical? Make several symmetrical designs with the tangrams. Draw in the lines of symmetry.

4) Design a set of tangram pieces of your own using some different shapes in the set. Make some figures with your shapes.

5) Present your principal with a difficult tangram puzzle. Give him a few days to figure it out.

TANGRAMATH ©1971 Creative Publications

PART THREE

EACH OF THE FIVE TANGRAM SHAPES BELOW CAN BE COVERED WITH THE SMALL TRIANGLE TANGRAM !

HOW MANY OF THE SMALL TANGRAM TRIANGLES COVER EACH FIGURE ?

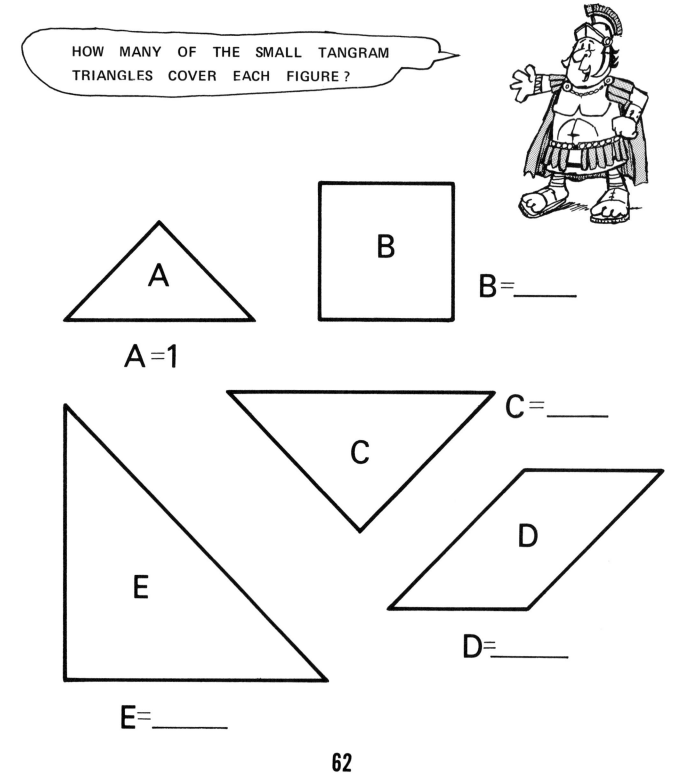

A = 1

B = _____

C = _____

D = _____

E = _____

AREA IS A MEASURE OF COVERING.

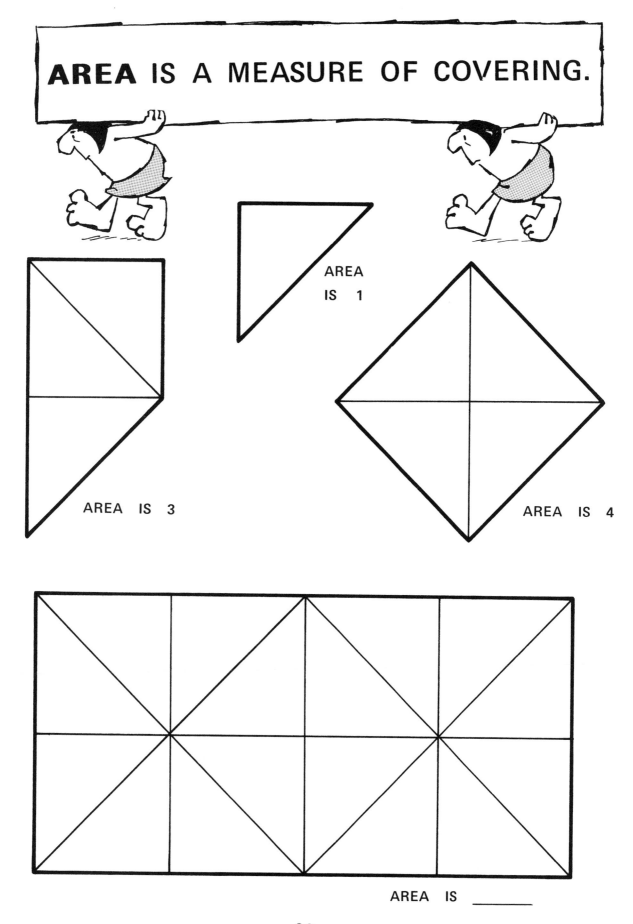

AREA IS 1

AREA IS 3

AREA IS 4

AREA IS _____

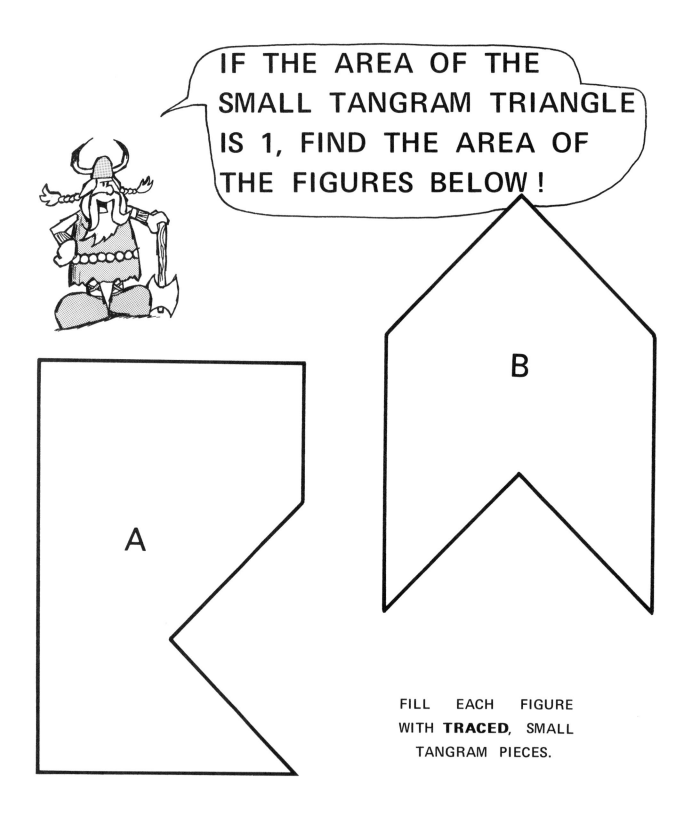

IF THE AREA OF THE SMALL TANGRAM TRIANGLE IS 1, FIND THE AREA OF THE FIGURES BELOW!

A

B

FILL EACH FIGURE WITH **TRACED**, SMALL TANGRAM PIECES.

AREA IS A MEASURE OF COVERING

HOW MANY OF THE SQUARE TANGRAM PIECES COVER EACH FIGURE BELOW?

A

B

C

D

FILL EACH FIGURE WITH **TRACED** TANGRAM SQUARES.

USE TANGRAMS TO SHOW THAT ALL THE FIGURES BELOW HAVE THE SAME AREA.

TANGRAMATH ©1971 Creative Publications

66

USE TANGRAMS

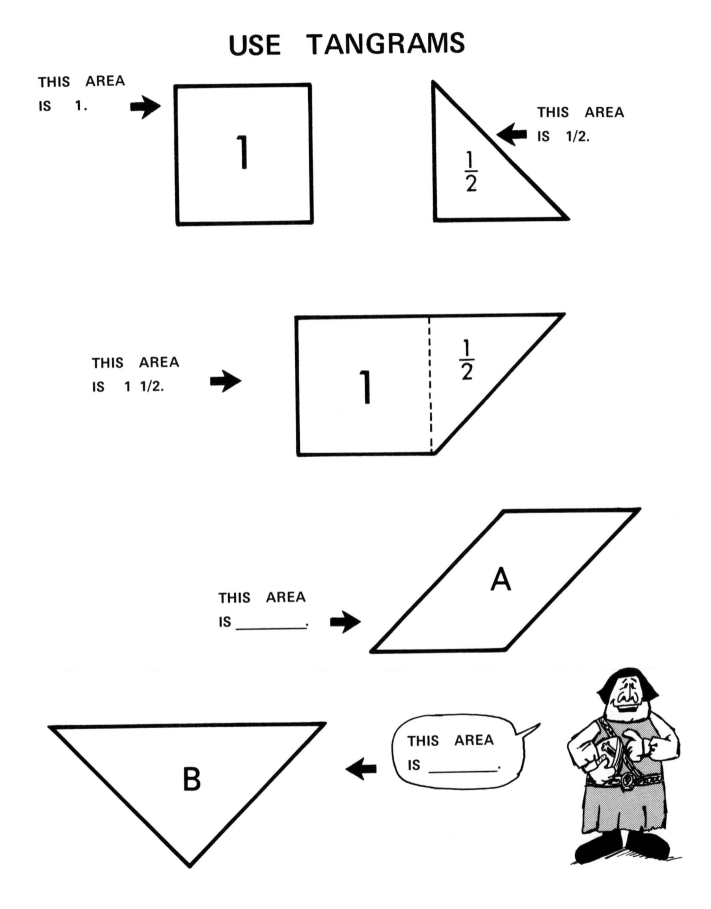

THIS AREA
IS 1.

THIS AREA
IS 1/2.

THIS AREA
IS 1 1/2.

THIS AREA
IS _____.

THIS AREA
IS _____.

USE TANGRAMS

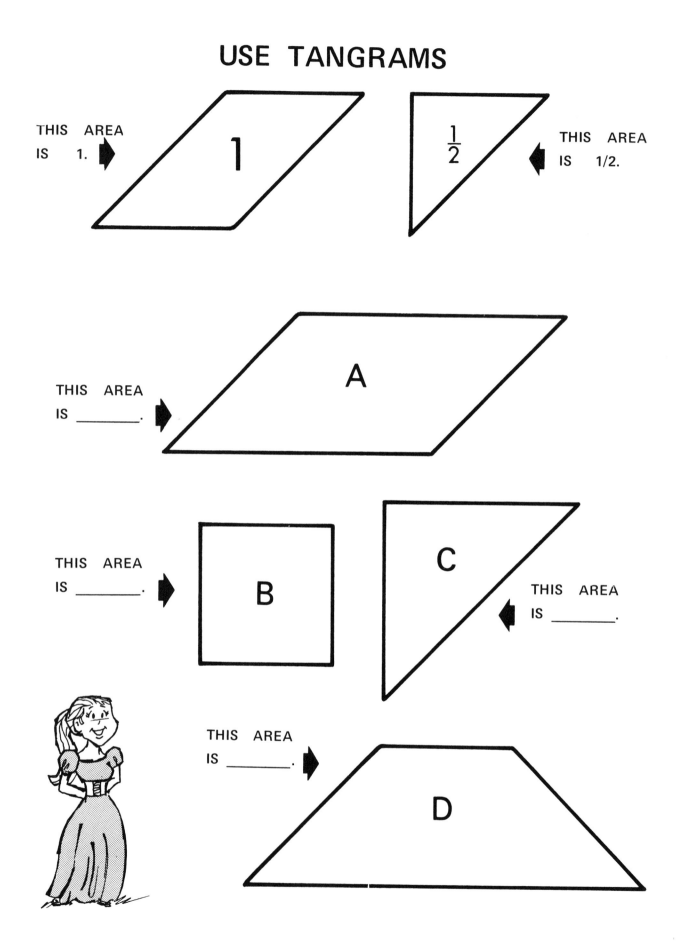

THIS AREA IS 1. ➤ **1**

◀ THIS AREA IS 1/2. **½**

THIS AREA IS _____. ➤ **A**

THIS AREA IS _____. ➤ **B**

C ◀ THIS AREA IS _____.

THIS AREA IS _____. ➤ **D**

USE TANGRAMS

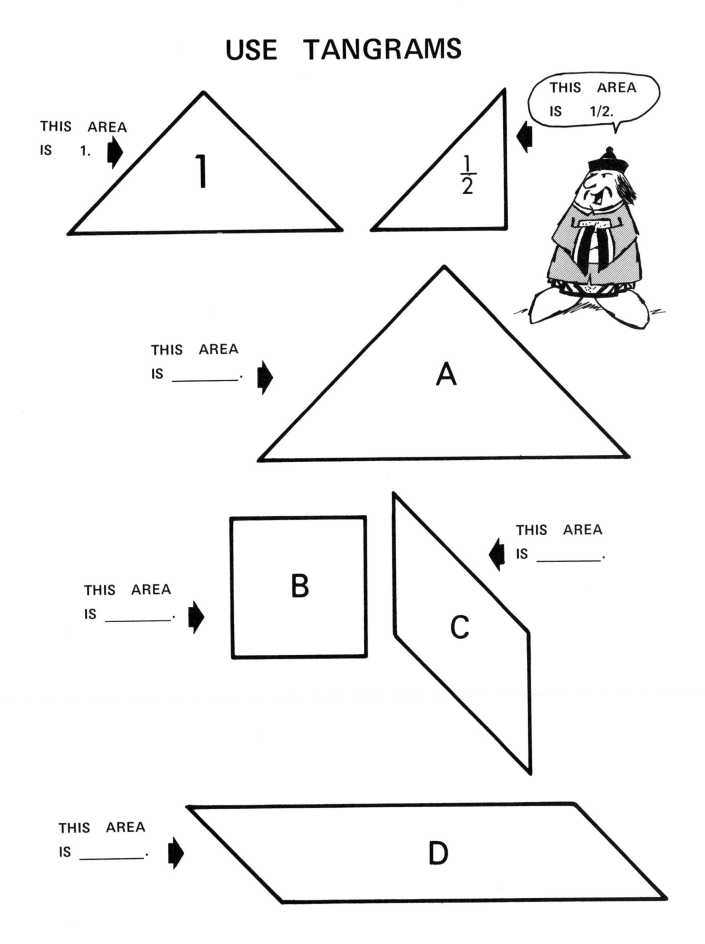

THIS AREA
IS   1.

1

THIS AREA
IS   1/2.

$\frac{1}{2}$

THIS AREA
IS _____.

A

THIS AREA
IS _____.

B

THIS AREA
IS _____.

C

THIS AREA
IS _____.

D

USE TANGRAMS

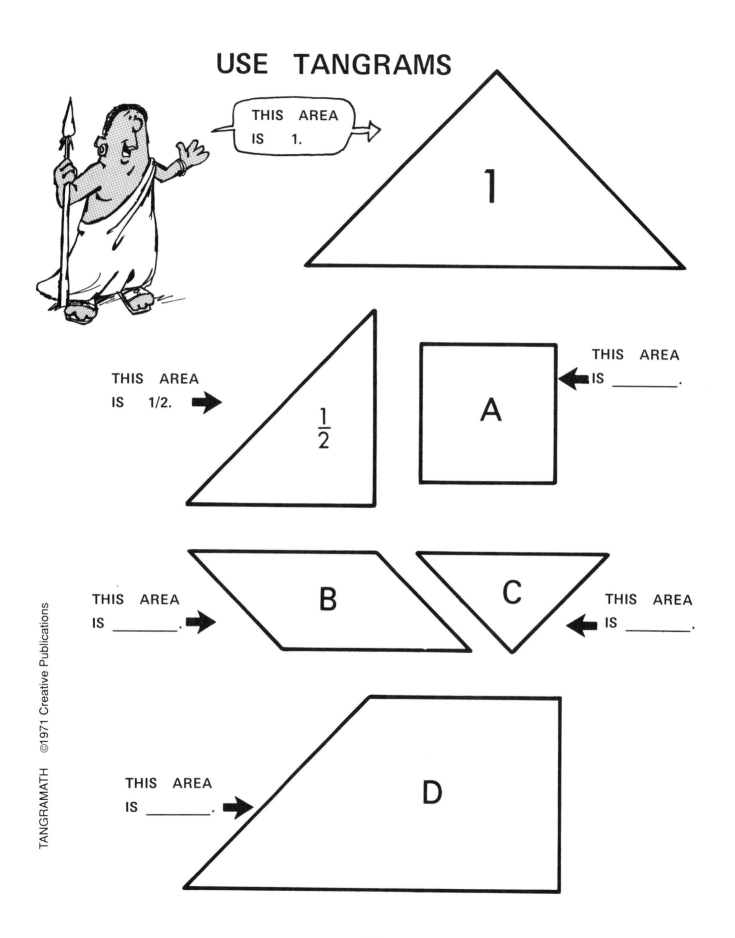

THIS AREA IS 1.

1

THIS AREA IS 1/2.

$\frac{1}{2}$

A

THIS AREA IS _____.

THIS AREA IS _____.

B

C

THIS AREA IS _____.

THIS AREA IS _____.

D

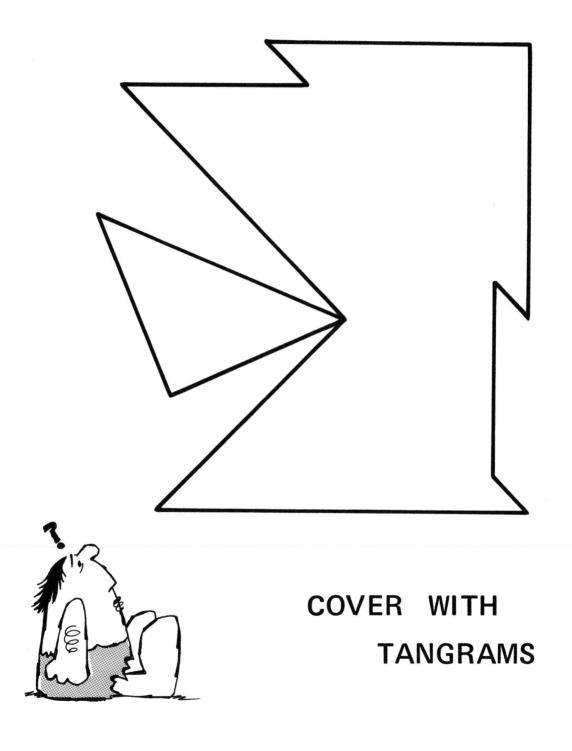

COVER WITH
TANGRAMS

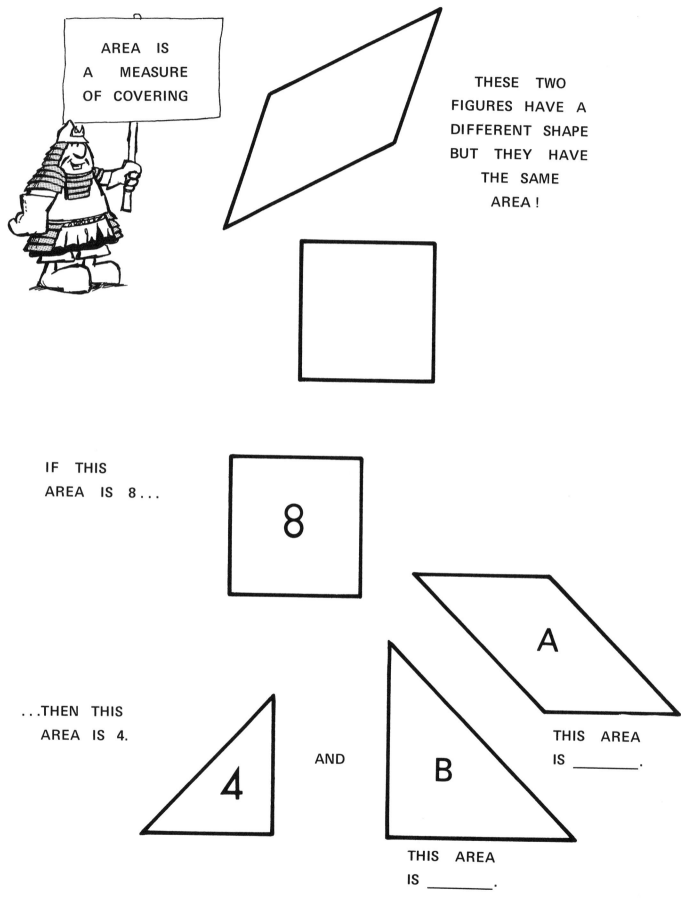

AREA IS A MEASURE OF COVERING

THESE TWO FIGURES HAVE A DIFFERENT SHAPE BUT THEY HAVE THE SAME AREA !

IF THIS AREA IS 8...

8

...THEN THIS AREA IS 4.

4

AND

B

A

THIS AREA IS _____.

THIS AREA IS _____.

CAN YOU FIT THE SQUARE TANGRAM IN THE TWO SHAPES BELOW?

NO! BUT THEY STILL HAVE THE SAME AREA!

WHICH TWO FIGURES HAVE THE SAME AREA?
USE TANGRAMS.

A

B

C

COVER EACH FIGURE (ONE AT A TIME)
WITH TANGRAMS TO TELL...

WHICH TWO FIGURES HAVE THE SAME AREA?

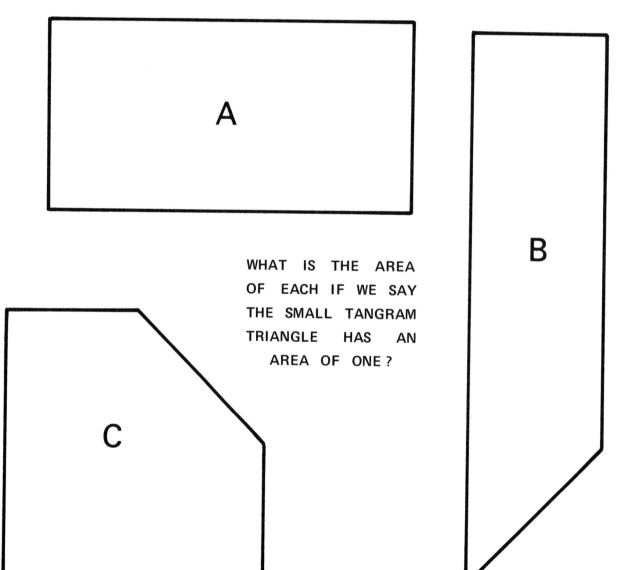

A

B

C

WHAT IS THE AREA
OF EACH IF WE SAY
THE SMALL TANGRAM
TRIANGLE HAS AN
AREA OF ONE?

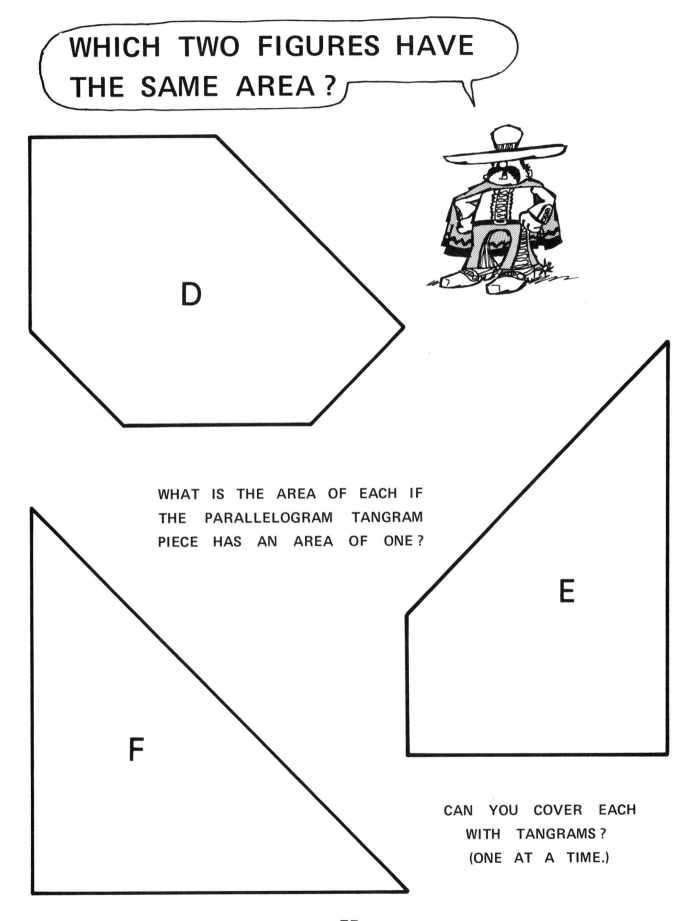

WHICH TWO FIGURES HAVE THE SAME AREA ?

D

WHAT IS THE AREA OF EACH IF THE PARALLELOGRAM TANGRAM PIECE HAS AN AREA OF ONE ?

E

F

CAN YOU COVER EACH WITH TANGRAMS ? (ONE AT A TIME.)

TANGRAMATH   ©1971 Creative Publications

75

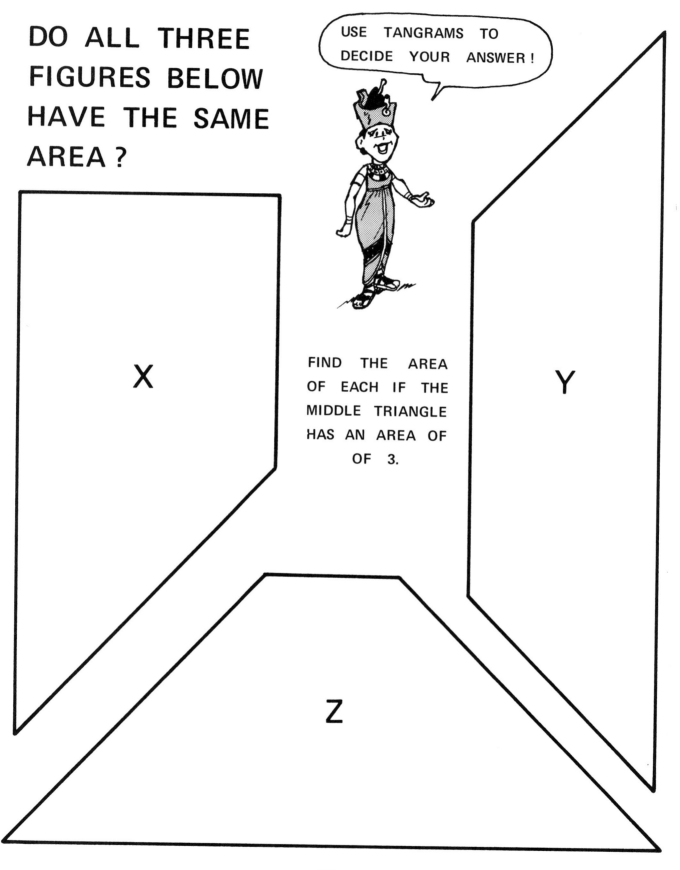

DO ALL THREE
FIGURES BELOW
HAVE THE SAME
AREA ?

USE TANGRAMS TO
DECIDE YOUR ANSWER !

X

Y

FIND THE AREA
OF EACH IF THE
MIDDLE TRIANGLE
HAS AN AREA OF
OF 3.

Z

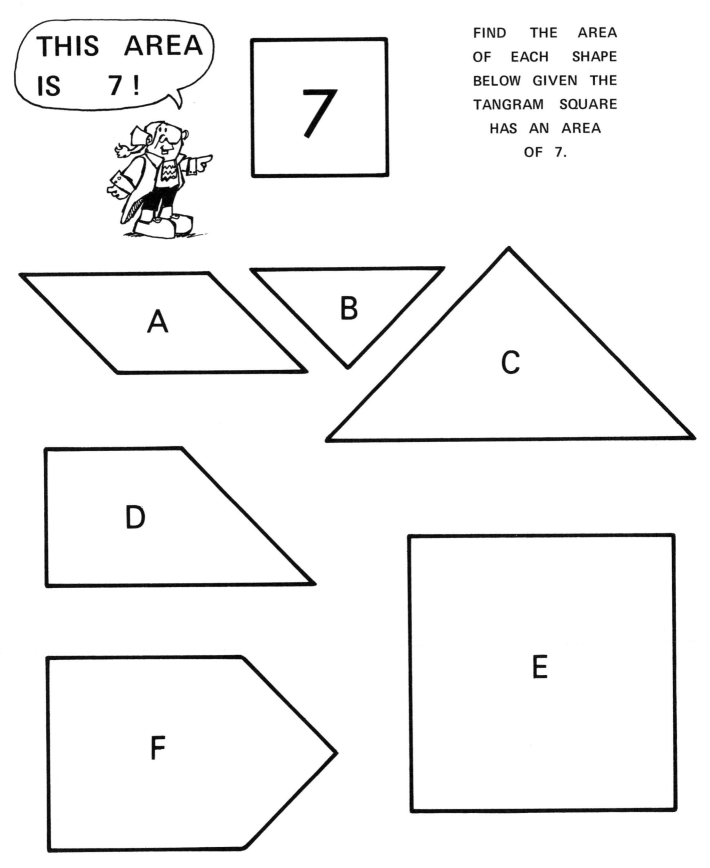

THIS AREA IS 7!

7

FIND THE AREA OF EACH SHAPE BELOW GIVEN THE TANGRAM SQUARE HAS AN AREA OF 7.

A

B

C

D

E

F

USE ALL SEVEN TANGRAMS
TO FORM THIS FIGURE!

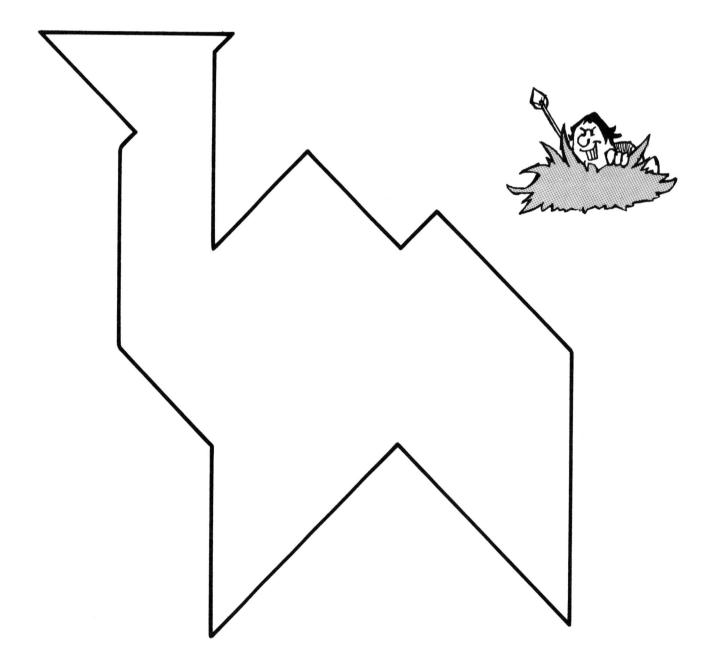

COULD YOU COVER THE SHADED REGION BELOW EXACTLY WITH TANGRAM PIECES?

DOES THE FIGURE BELOW HAVE AN AREA?

WOULD THE AREA BE HARD TO FIGURE?

TRACE AS MANY TANGRAM SQUARES IN THE REGION AS YOU CAN. HOW MANY "FULL" SQUARES DID YOU FIT IN?

IF YOU WERE GOING TO COVER A FLOOR WITH TILES. WHICH WOULD BE THE BEST; CIRCLES ? SQUARES ?

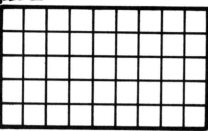 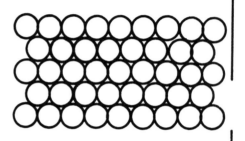

TRY TO MEASURE THE AREA OF THIS ENTIRE SHEET OF PAPER BY COVERING IT WITH TRACED TANGRAM SQUARES.

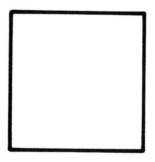

WOULD THE TANGRAM PARALLELOGRAM OR THE SMALL TRIANGLE TANGRAM BE EASIER FOR MEASURING ?

AREA IS A MEASURE OF COVERING.

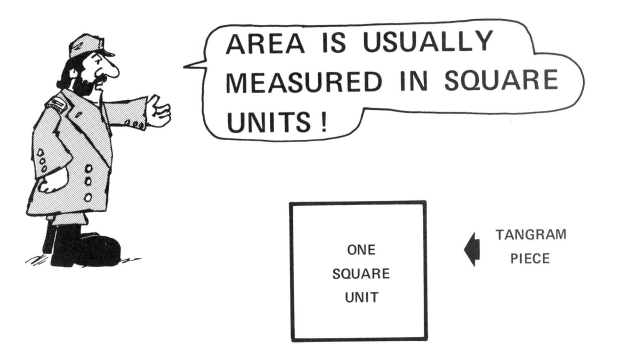

AREA IS USUALLY MEASURED IN SQUARE UNITS !

ONE SQUARE UNIT

TANGRAM PIECE

EACH EDGE OF THE SQUARE IS ONE UNIT LONG.

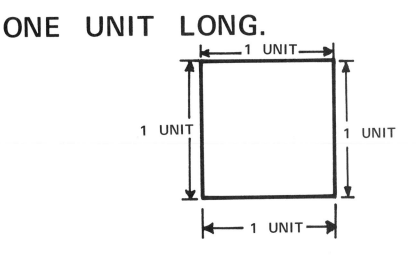

1 UNIT

1 UNIT

1 UNIT

1 UNIT

THE SUM OF THE EDGES IS 4 UNITS, BUT THE AREA IS _____ SQUARE UNIT.

AREA OF A RECTANGLE

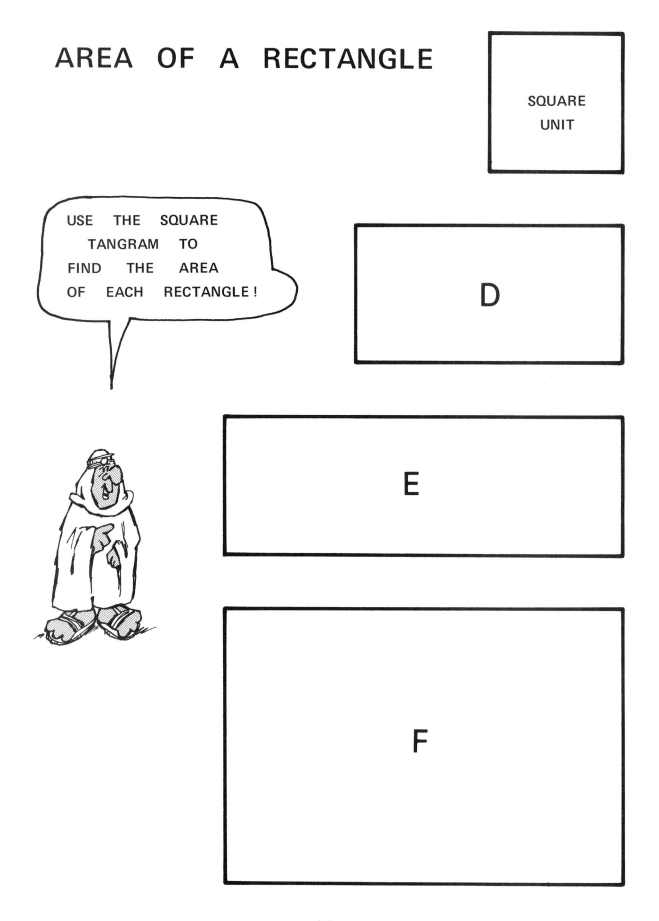

SQUARE
UNIT

USE THE SQUARE TANGRAM TO FIND THE AREA OF EACH RECTANGLE!

D

E

F

AREA OF A RECTANGLE

(LENGTH X WIDTH)

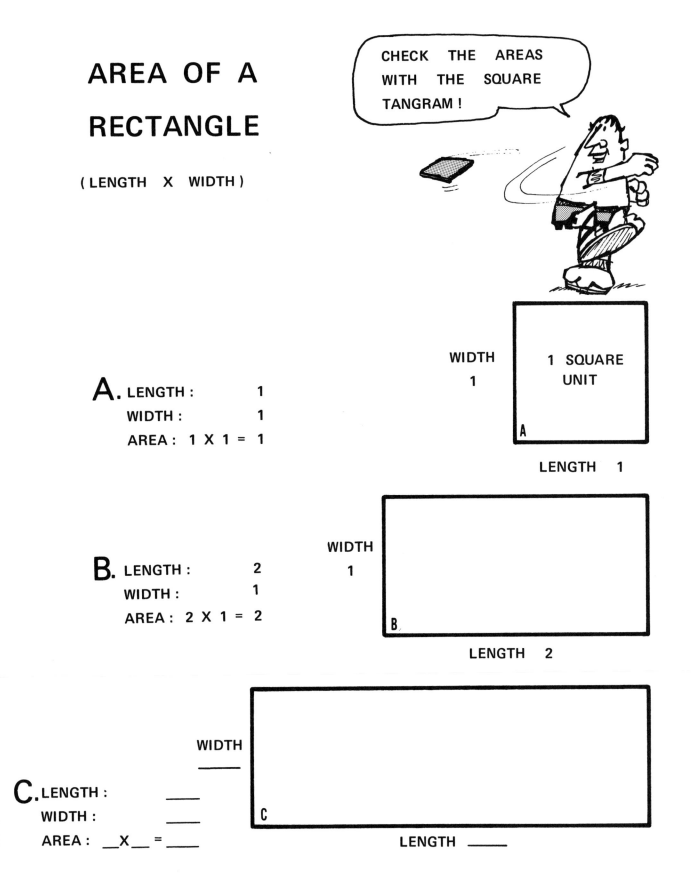

CHECK THE AREAS WITH THE SQUARE TANGRAM !

WIDTH
1

1 SQUARE UNIT

A

LENGTH   1

A. LENGTH :   1
WIDTH :   1
AREA : 1 X 1 = 1

WIDTH
1

B

LENGTH   2

B. LENGTH :   2
WIDTH :   1
AREA : 2 X 1 = 2

WIDTH
_____

C

LENGTH _____

C. LENGTH :   _____
WIDTH :   _____
AREA : __ X __ = _____

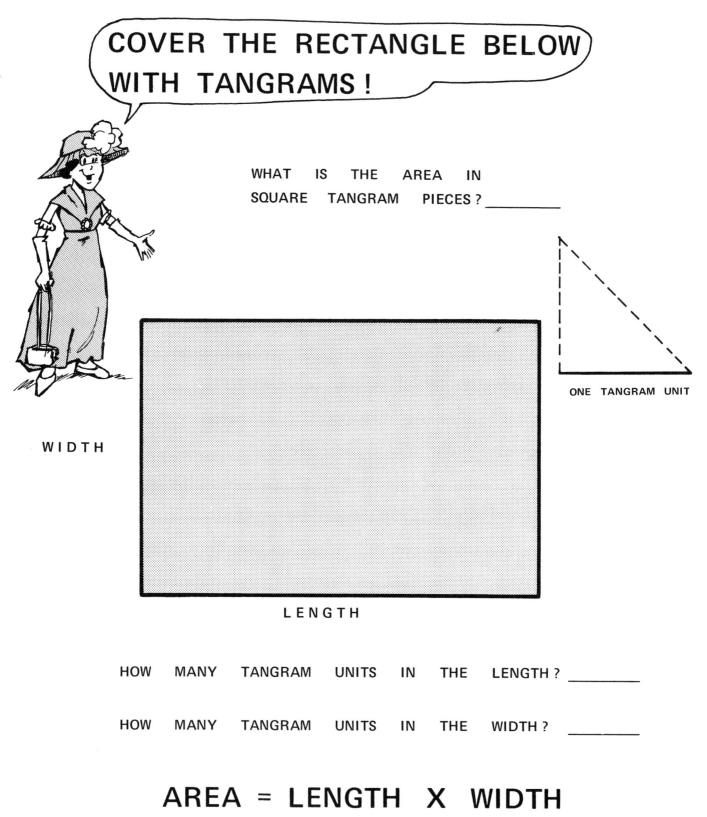

COVER THE RECTANGLE BELOW WITH TANGRAMS!

WHAT IS THE AREA IN SQUARE TANGRAM PIECES? _____

ONE TANGRAM UNIT

WIDTH

LENGTH

HOW MANY TANGRAM UNITS IN THE LENGTH? _____

HOW MANY TANGRAM UNITS IN THE WIDTH? _____

AREA = LENGTH X WIDTH

SHOWN BELOW IS ONE SQUARE INCH

DOES THE SQUARE TANGRAM PIECE FIT EXACTLY ON THE SQUARE INCH? ____

1″

1″ 1″

1″

COVER THE SQUARE EXACTLY WITH ALL SEVEN TANGRAM PIECES. WHAT IS THE AREA IN TANGRAM SQUARES? (IT IS NOT 16.)

4 INCHES

4″ 4″

4″

16 SQUARE INCHES

COVER WITH
TANGRAM TRIANGLES

THEN MOVE ONE
TRIANGLE ABOVE AND
MAKE A PARALLELOGRAM
LIKE THIS

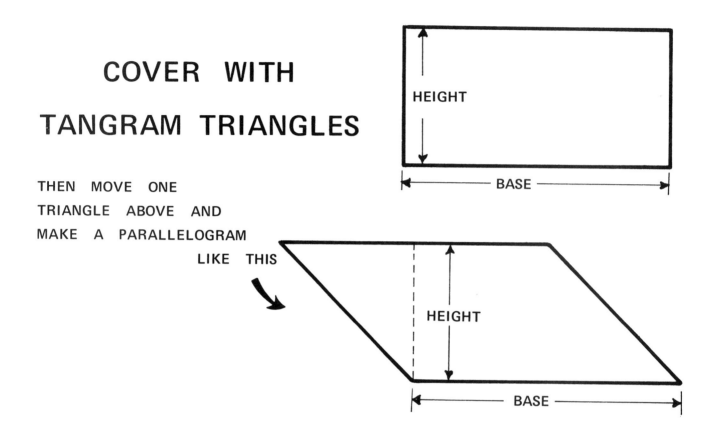

HEIGHT

BASE

HEIGHT

BASE

ARE THE BASES OF THE
RECTANGLE AND THE
PARALLELOGRAM CON—
GRUENT ?

ARE THE HEIGHTS CONGRUENT ?

ARE THE AREAS THE SAME ?

TANGRAMATH   ©1971 Creative Publications

IN THE PARALLELOGRAM BELOW...

WHICH IS LONGER, THE SIDE OR THE HEIGHT?

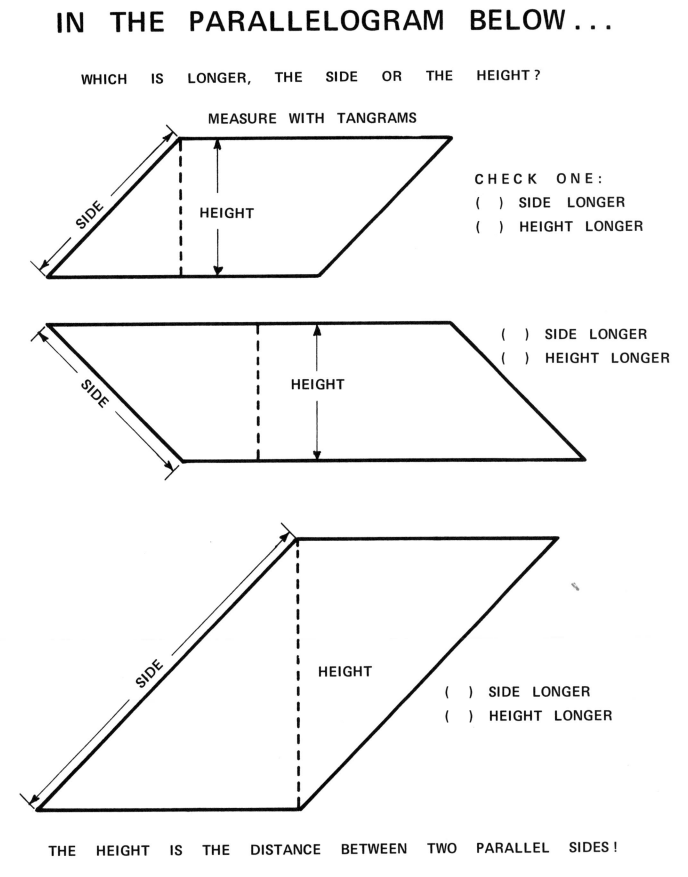

MEASURE WITH TANGRAMS

SIDE

HEIGHT

CHECK ONE:
( ) SIDE LONGER
( ) HEIGHT LONGER

SIDE

HEIGHT

( ) SIDE LONGER
( ) HEIGHT LONGER

SIDE

HEIGHT

( ) SIDE LONGER
( ) HEIGHT LONGER

THE HEIGHT IS THE DISTANCE BETWEEN TWO PARALLEL SIDES!

TANGRAMATH   ©1971 Creative Publications

AREA OF A PARALLELOGRAM

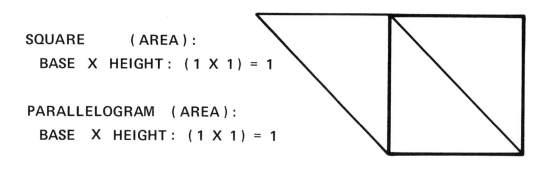

SQUARE   (AREA):
    BASE X HEIGHT : (1 X 1) = 1

PARALLELOGRAM   (AREA):
    BASE   X   HEIGHT : (1 X 1) = 1

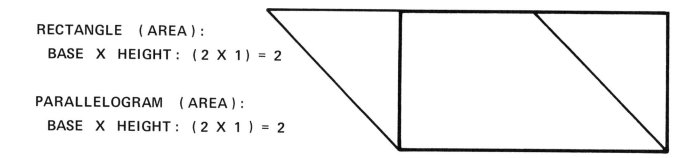

RECTANGLE   (AREA):
    BASE   X   HEIGHT : (2 X 1) = 2

PARALLELOGRAM   (AREA):
    BASE   X   HEIGHT : (2 X 1) = 2

USE YOUR TANGRAM PIECES TO DRAW A PICTURE LIKE THE ONES ABOVE SHOWING A RECTANGLE WITH BASE MEASURING 3 UNITS AND HEIGHT MEASURING 1 UNIT HAS THE SAME AREA AS A PARALLELOGRAM WITH A BASE OF 3 UNITS AND A HEIGHT OF 1 UNIT.

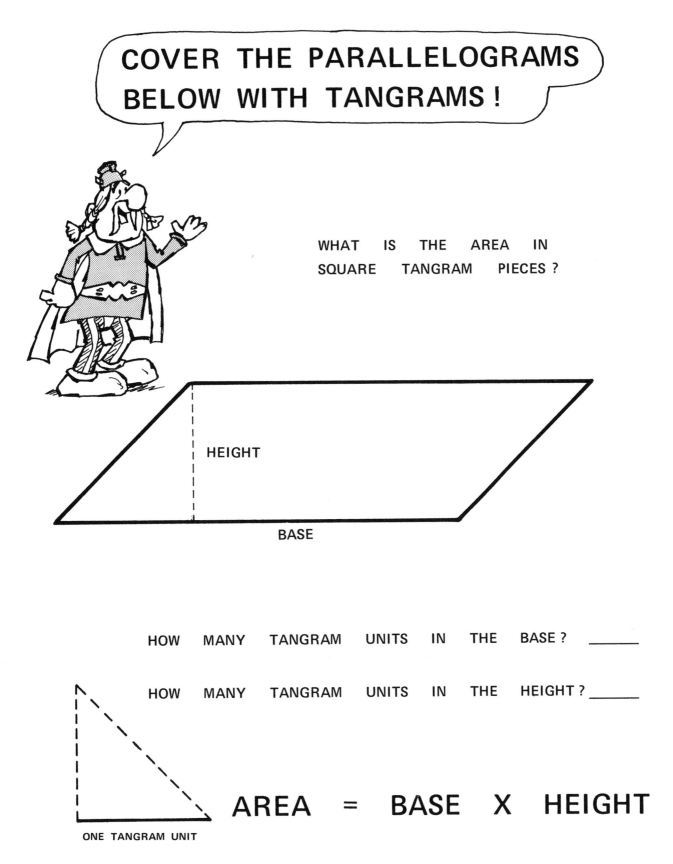

COVER THE PARALLELOGRAMS BELOW WITH TANGRAMS!

WHAT IS THE AREA IN SQUARE TANGRAM PIECES?

HEIGHT

BASE

HOW MANY TANGRAM UNITS IN THE BASE? _____

HOW MANY TANGRAM UNITS IN THE HEIGHT? _____

ONE TANGRAM UNIT

AREA = BASE X HEIGHT

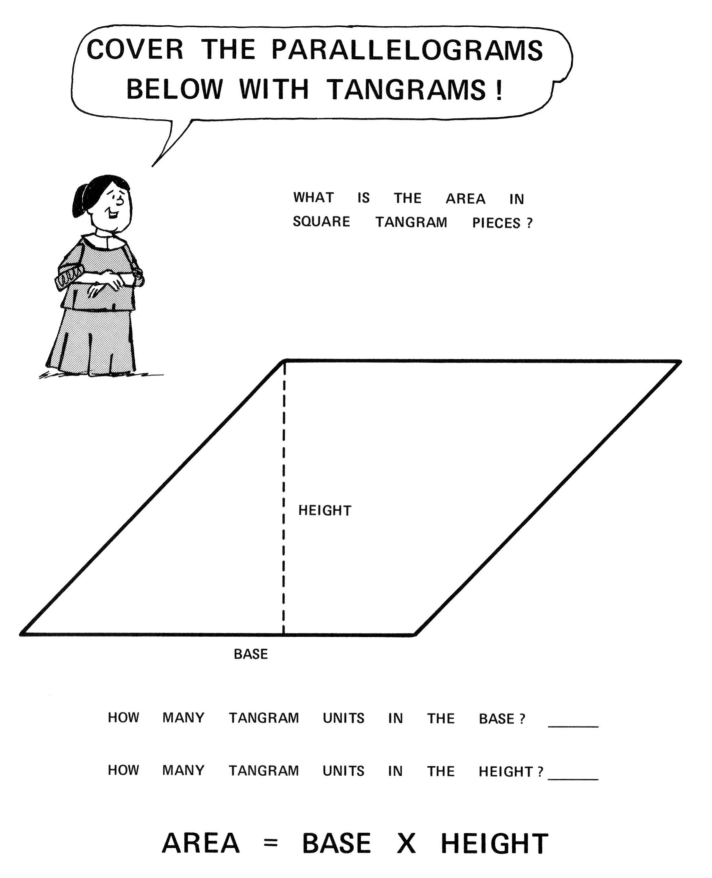

COVER THE PARALLELOGRAMS BELOW WITH TANGRAMS!

WHAT IS THE AREA IN SQUARE TANGRAM PIECES?

HEIGHT

BASE

HOW MANY TANGRAM UNITS IN THE BASE? _____

HOW MANY TANGRAM UNITS IN THE HEIGHT? _____

AREA = BASE X HEIGHT

CAN YOU FORM EACH OF
THESE SHAPES WITH ALL
SEVEN TANGRAM PIECES?

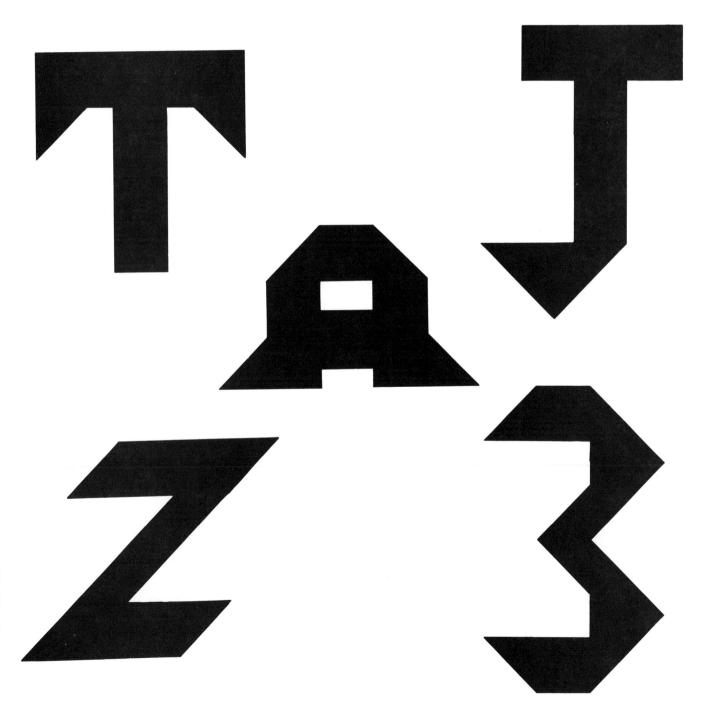

IN EACH OF THE FIGURES BELOW, THE SHADED TRIANGLE IS WHAT PART OF THE PARALLELOGRAM?

_____

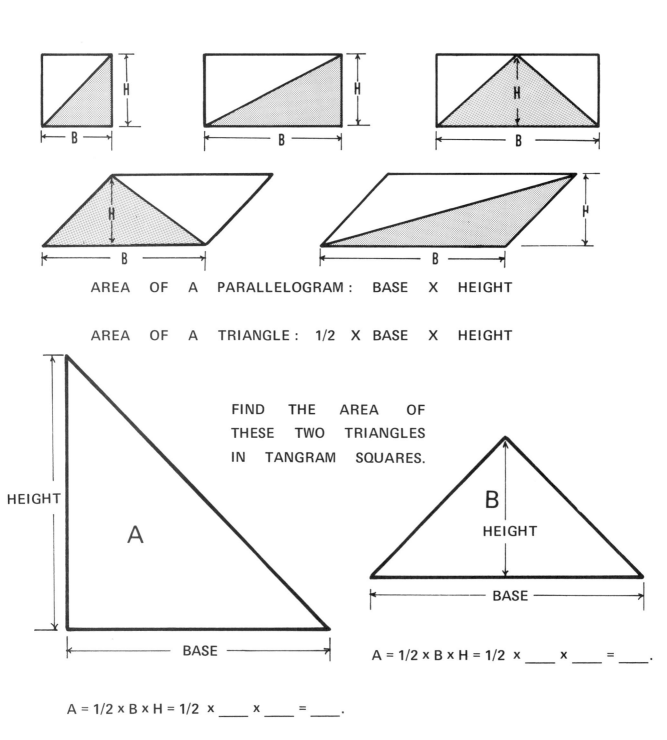

AREA OF A PARALLELOGRAM: BASE X HEIGHT

AREA OF A TRIANGLE: 1/2 X BASE X HEIGHT

FIND THE AREA OF THESE TWO TRIANGLES IN TANGRAM SQUARES.

A = 1/2 x B x H = 1/2 x ____ x ____ = ____.

A = 1/2 x B x H = 1/2 x ____ x ____ = ____.

AREA OF A TRIANGLE (1/2 BASE X HEIGHT)

COVER THE TRIANGLE
BELOW WITH TANGRAMS.

WHAT IS THE AREA
IN SQUARE TANGRAM
PIECES ? _____

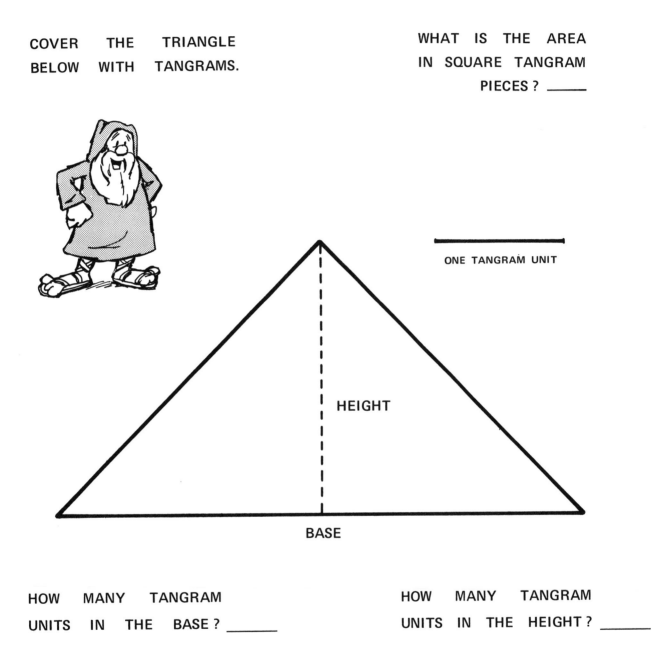

ONE TANGRAM UNIT

HEIGHT

BASE

HOW MANY TANGRAM
UNITS IN THE BASE ? _____

HOW MANY TANGRAM
UNITS IN THE HEIGHT ? _____

AREA= 1/2 X BASE X HEIGHT

USING THE TANGRAM PIECES CAN YOU MAKE TRIANGLES WHOSE AREAS MEASURE:

1/2, 1 1/2, 2, 3, 4, 5, 6 AND 8 SQUARE TANGRAM UNITS?

ASSEMBLE THEM
HERE !

SOME   MAY   NOT   BE   POSSIBLE.

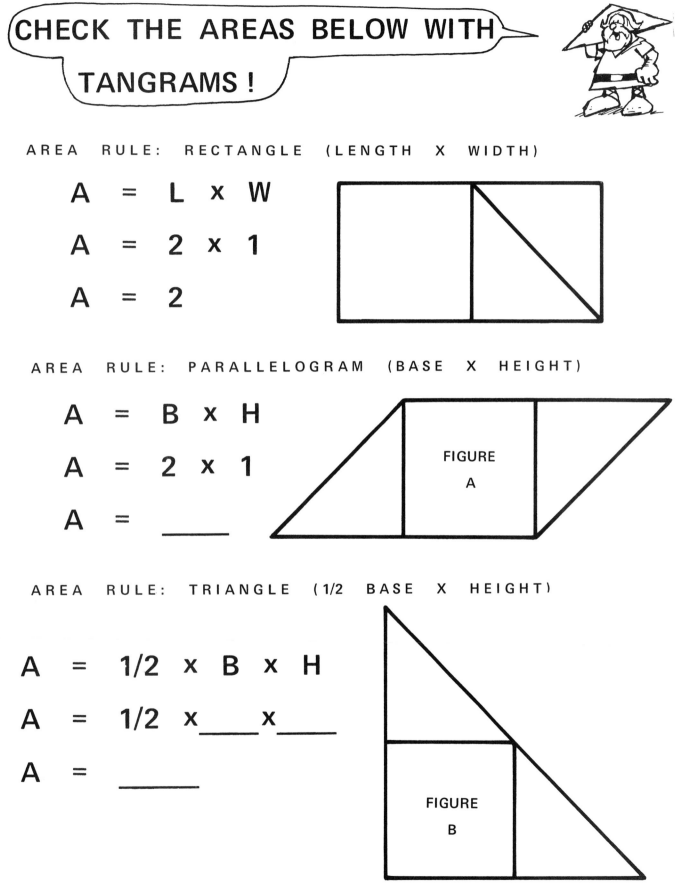

CHECK THE AREAS BELOW WITH TANGRAMS !

AREA RULE: RECTANGLE (LENGTH X WIDTH)

A = L x W

A = 2 x 1

A = 2

AREA RULE: PARALLELOGRAM (BASE X HEIGHT)

A = B x H

A = 2 x 1

A = _____

FIGURE A

AREA RULE: TRIANGLE (1/2 BASE X HEIGHT)

A = 1/2 x B x H

A = 1/2 x ___ x ___

A = _____

FIGURE B

TANGRAMATH   ©1971 Creative Publications

CAN YOU FORM EACH OF THESE SHAPES WITH ALL SEVEN TANGRAM PIECES?

TRAPEZOIDS

A TRAPEZOID IS A FOUR SIDED FIGURE WITH TWO SIDES PARALLEL AND TWO SIDES NON—PARALLEL

COVER THE TRAPEZOID WITH TANGRAMS.

TANGRAMATH

THE PARALLEL SIDES OF A TRAPEZOID ARE CALLED
ITS BASES. EVERY TRAPEZOID HAS TWO BASES. WHICH
LINE SEGMENTS ARE BASES OF THE TRAPEZOIDS BELOW?

TRAPEZOID A B C D,   BASES : _____ AND _____

TRAPEZOID E F G H,   BASES : _____ AND _____

TRAPEZOID I J K L,   BASES : _____ AND _____

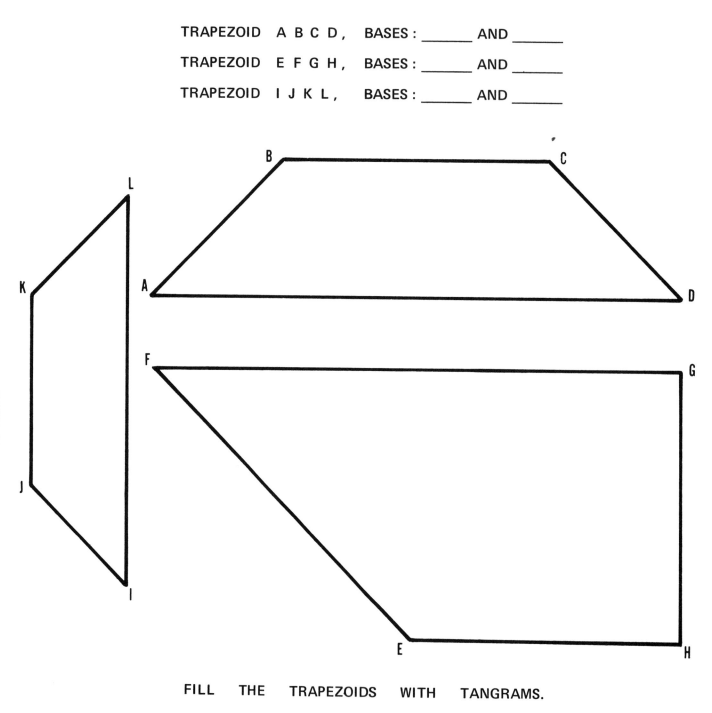

FILL   THE   TRAPEZOIDS   WITH   TANGRAMS.

COVER THE RECTANGLE BELOW
WITH TANGRAM PIECES.

MOVE ONE PIECE TO MAKE A TRAPEZOID.

HAS THE SHAPE OF THE FIGURE CHANGED? _____

HAS THE AREA OF THE FIGURE CHANGED? _____

COVER THE TRAPEZOID BELOW
WITH TANGRAMS.

WHAT IS ITS AREA IN TANGRAM SQUARES?

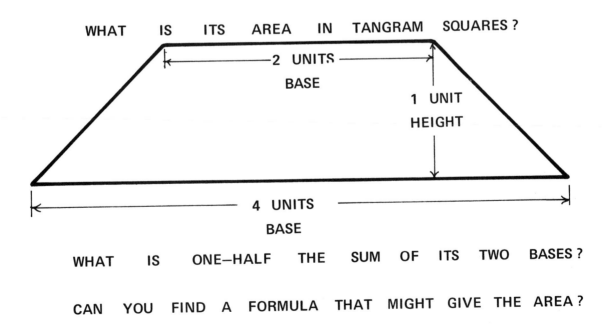

2 UNITS
BASE

1 UNIT
HEIGHT

4 UNITS
BASE

WHAT IS ONE—HALF THE SUM OF ITS TWO BASES?

CAN YOU FIND A FORMULA THAT MIGHT GIVE THE AREA?

AREA OF A TRAPEZOID

AREA = 1/2 X (SUM OF BASES) X HEIGHT

1. IS THE FIGURE BELOW A TRAPEZOID?

2. CAN YOU COVER IT WITH TANGRAMS?

3. WHAT IS THE LENGTH OF ITS LOWER BASE (TANGRAM UNITS)? _____

4. WHAT IS THE LENGTH OF ITS UPPER BASE (TANGRAM UNITS)? _____

5. WHAT IS ITS HEIGHT (TANGRAM UNITS)?

6. WHAT IS ITS AREA IN TANGRAM SQUARES? (USE THE FORMULA ABOVE, THEN CHECK YOUR ANSWER BY COUNTING.)

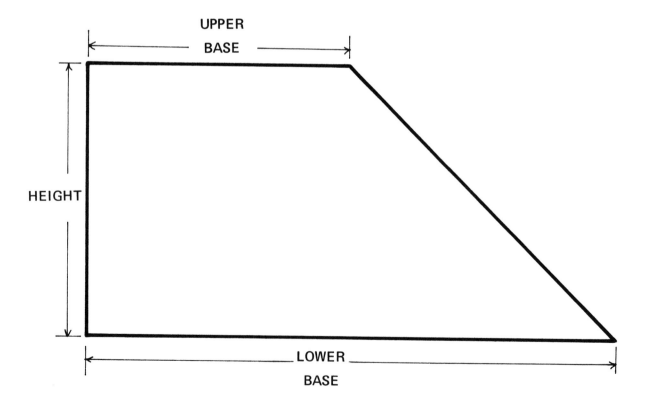

USE THESE THREE TANGRAM SHAPES
TO MAKE:

    1. A SQUARE

    2. A TRIANGLE

    3. A PARALLELOGRAM

    4. A TRAPEZOID

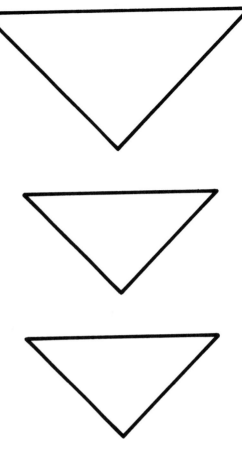

USE THESE THREE TANGRAM SHAPES
TO MAKE:

    1. A RECTANGLE

    2. A TRIANGLE

    3. A PARALLELOGRAM

    4. A TRAPEZOID

CAN YOU FIGURE OUT A "SNEAKY"
WAY TO MAKE A SQUARE?

USE THESE FOUR TANGRAM SHAPES TO MAKE:

1. A SQUARE

2. A PARALLELOGRAM

3. A TRAPEZOID

4. A RECTANGLE

5. A TRIANGLE

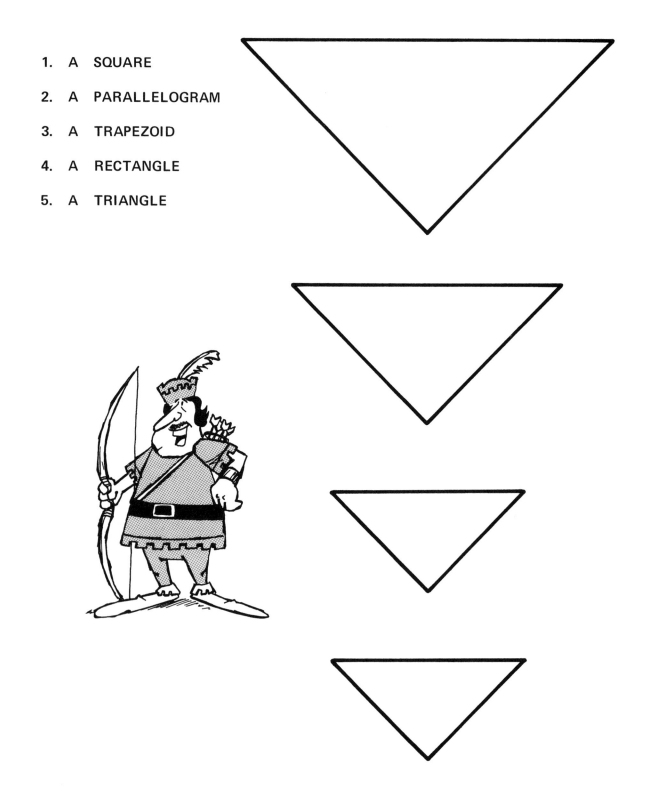

TANGRAMATH   ©1971 Creative Publications

CAN YOU FORM EACH OF THESE SHAPES WITH ALL SEVEN TANGRAM PIECES?

USE THESE THREE TANGRAM SHAPES
TO MAKE :

    1. A RECTANGLE

    2. A TRIANGLE

    3. TWO DIFFERENT PARALLELOGRAMS

    4. A TRAPEZOID

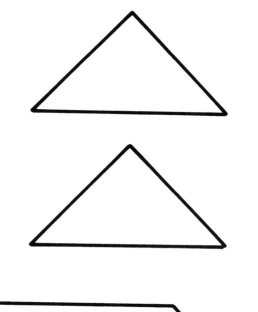

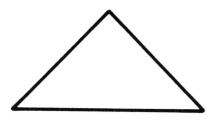

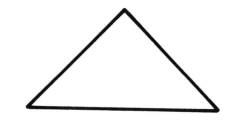

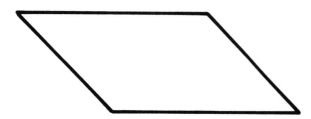

USE THESE FOUR TANGRAM SHAPES
TO MAKE :

    1. A RECTANGLE

    2. A PARALLELOGRAM

    3. A TRAPEZOID

    4. A PENTAGON (5 SIDES)

    5. A HEXAGON (6 SIDES)

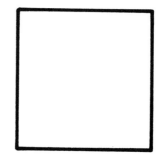

USING ALL OF THE SEVEN TANGRAM PIECES EXCEPT THE TWO LARGE TRIANGLES FORM:

1. A TRIANGLE

2. A SQUARE

3. A RECTANGLE (NOT SQUARE)

4. A PARALLELOGRAM

5. A TRAPEZOID

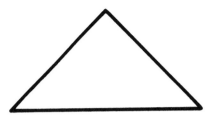

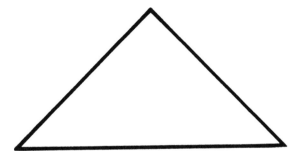

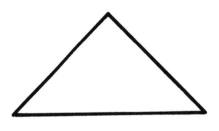

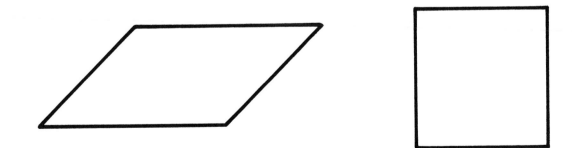

IF A LINE JOINING TWO VERTICES OF A POLYGON LIES OUTSIDE THE POLYGON, THE POLYGON IS **CONCAVE**.

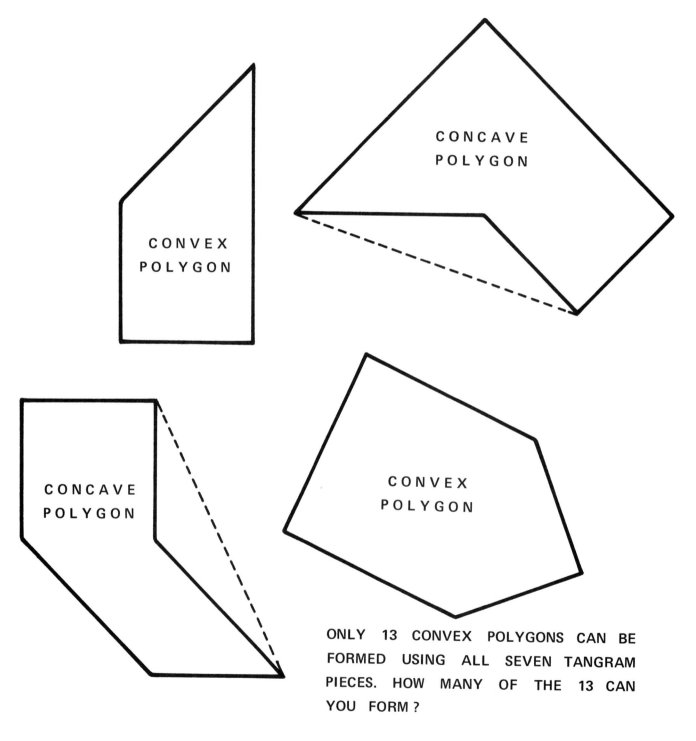

CONVEX POLYGON

CONCAVE POLYGON

CONCAVE POLYGON

CONVEX POLYGON

ONLY 13 CONVEX POLYGONS CAN BE FORMED USING ALL SEVEN TANGRAM PIECES. HOW MANY OF THE 13 CAN YOU FORM?

THE PYTHAGOREAN THEOREM IS A VALUABLE RULE WHICH IS VERY USEFUL IN SOLVING MANY TYPES OF PROBLEMS. ON THE NEXT SEVERAL PAGES YOU WILL SEE HOW THE PYTHAGOREAN THEOREM HELPS YOU IN SOLVING CERTAIN TANGRAM PUZZLES. THE RULE STATES:

IN A RIGHT TRIANGLE, THE SQUARE OF THE HYPOTENUSE IS EQUAL TO THE SUM OF THE SQUARES OF THE OTHER TWO SIDES.

EXAMPLES:

(HYPOTENUSE)

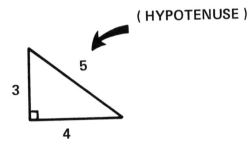

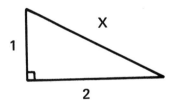

$$3^2 + 4^2 = 5^2$$

$$9 + 16 = 25$$

$$1^2 + 2^2 = X^2$$

$$1 + 4 = X^2$$

$$5 = X^2$$

$$X = \sqrt{5}$$

(Square root of five*)

*Note: $\sqrt{5} \times \sqrt{5} = 5$

THE SMALL TANGRAM TRIANGLE IS A RIGHT TRIANGLE. IF WE AGREE THAT THE TWO SIDES OF THE RIGHT ANGLE MEASURE ONE UNIT THEN WE CAN FIND THE MEASURE OF THE HYPOTENUSE BY USING THE PYTHAGOREAN THEOREM.

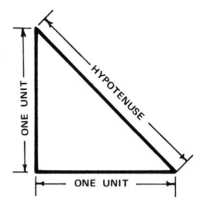

NAMELY,

$$1^2 \; + \; 1^2 \; = \; X^2$$
$$1 \; + \; 1 \; = \; X^2$$
$$2 \; = \; X^2$$

$$\text{SO} \quad X \; = \; \sqrt{2} \;, \quad \text{BECAUSE} \quad \sqrt{2} \; \times \; \sqrt{2} \; = \; 2$$

COMPLETE THE LABELING BELOW:

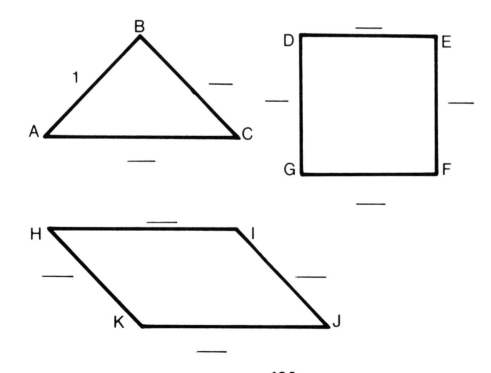

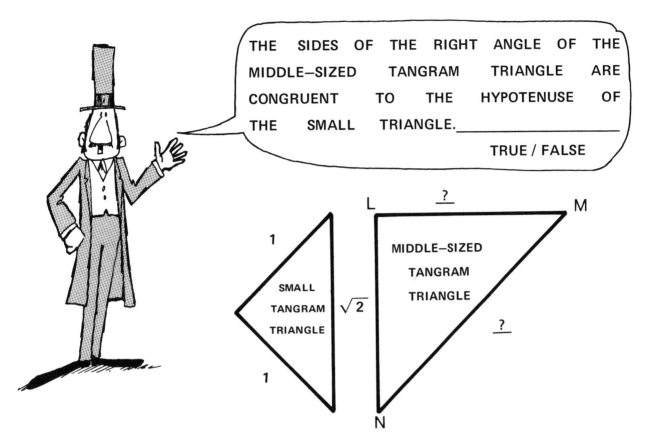

THE SIDES OF THE RIGHT ANGLE OF THE MIDDLE—SIZED TANGRAM TRIANGLE ARE CONGRUENT TO THE HYPOTENUSE OF THE SMALL TRIANGLE._____

TRUE / FALSE

USE THE PYTHAGOREAN THEOREM TO FIND THE HYPOTENUSE OF THE MIDDLE—SIZED TANGRAM TRIANGLE.

_____

_____

_____

_____

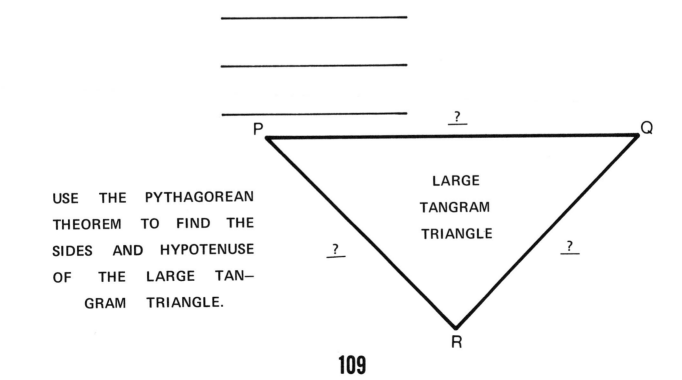

USE THE PYTHAGOREAN THEOREM TO FIND THE SIDES AND HYPOTENUSE OF THE LARGE TAN—GRAM TRIANGLE.

USING THE DIMENSIONS BELOW, FIND THE PERIMETERS
AREAS OF EACH OF THE TANGRAM PIECES.

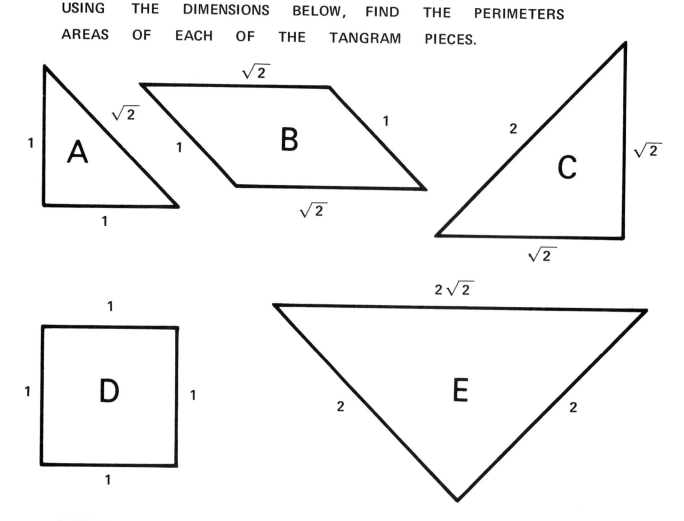

NOTICE THAT WE LABELED THE HYPOTENUSE OF THE LARGE
TANGRAM TRIANGLE AS $2\sqrt{2}$ INSTEAD OF $\sqrt{8}$. $2\sqrt{2} = \sqrt{8}$
BECAUSE: $\sqrt{8} = \sqrt{4 \times 2} = \sqrt{4} \times \sqrt{2} = 2 \times \sqrt{2}$ OR SIMPLY $2\sqrt{2}$
(WHICH IS READ "TWO TIMES THE SQUARE ROOT OF TWO".)

PERIMETERS

A = _____ UNITS

B = _____ UNITS

C = _____ UNITS

D = _____ UNITS

E = _____ UNITS

AREAS

A = _____ SQUARE UNITS

B = _____ SQUARE UNITS

C = _____ SQUARE UNITS

D = _____ SQUARE UNITS

E = _____ SQUARE UNITS

FIND THE LENGTH OF EACH SIDE OF THE
FIGURES BELOW IN TANGRAM UNITS:

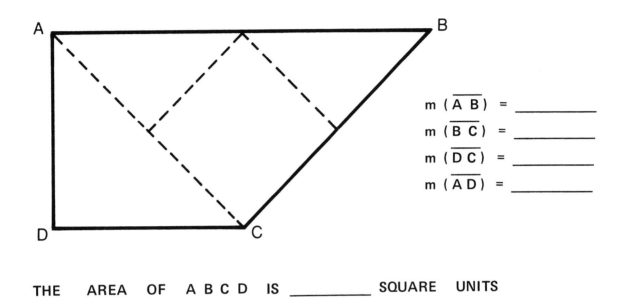

m ($\overline{A\ B}$) = _____

m ($\overline{B\ C}$) = _____

m ($\overline{D\ C}$) = _____

m ($\overline{A\ D}$) = _____

THE AREA OF A B C D IS _____ SQUARE UNITS

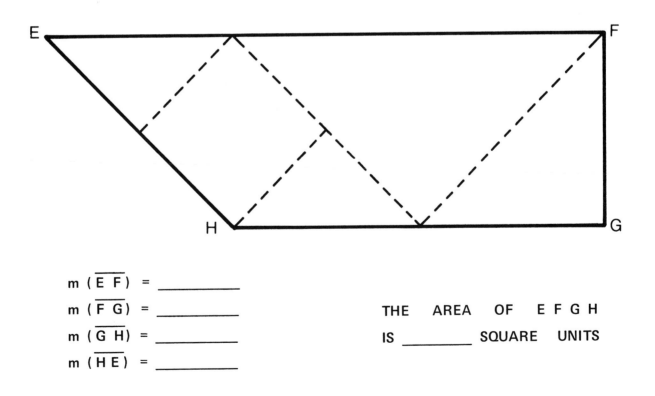

m ($\overline{E\ F}$) = _____

m ($\overline{F\ G}$) = _____

m ($\overline{G\ H}$) = _____

m ($\overline{H\ E}$) = _____

THE AREA OF E F G H
IS _____ SQUARE UNITS

TANGRAMATH   ©1971 Creative Publications

FORM A SQUARE USING THE TWO SMALL TANGRAM TRIANGLES AND ONE LARGE TANGRAM TRIANGLE.

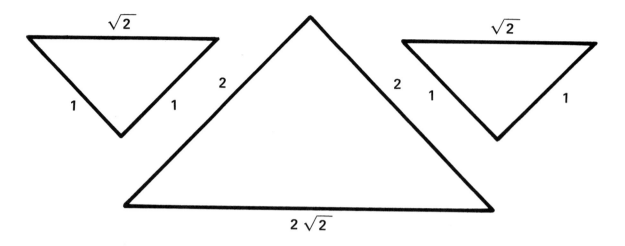

THERE ARE TWO WAYS TO APPROACH THIS PROBLEM:

1 TRIAL AND ERROR

TRY UNTIL YOU SUCCEED. IF YOU DON'T SUCCEED YOU AS— SUME IT CAN'T BE DONE. WHEN YOU SAY IT CAN'T BE DONE, YOU <u>HOPE</u> YOU ARE RIGHT.

2 AREA – PYTHAGOREAN THEOREM

1) FIGURE THE TOTAL AREA (AREA ABOVE WOULD BE 1/2 + 1/2 + 2 OR 3)

2) IF YOU KNOW THE AREA, THE LENGTH OF THE SIDE OF THE SQUARE WOULD BE THE SQUARE ROOT OF THE AREA. (IN THIS PROBLEM THE SIDE WOULD HAVE TO BE $\sqrt{3}$, BECAUSE $\sqrt{3} \times \sqrt{3} = 3$.)

3) COMBINE LENGTHS THAT MAKE THE REQUIRED SIDE (NO WAY TO FORM $\sqrt{3}$ FROM COMBINATIONS OF 1, $\sqrt{2}$, 2, $2\sqrt{2}$. CONCLUSION: A SQUARE CANNOT BE MADE FROM THESE PIECES.

FORM A SQUARE USING THE TANGRAM PIECES SHOWN BELOW:

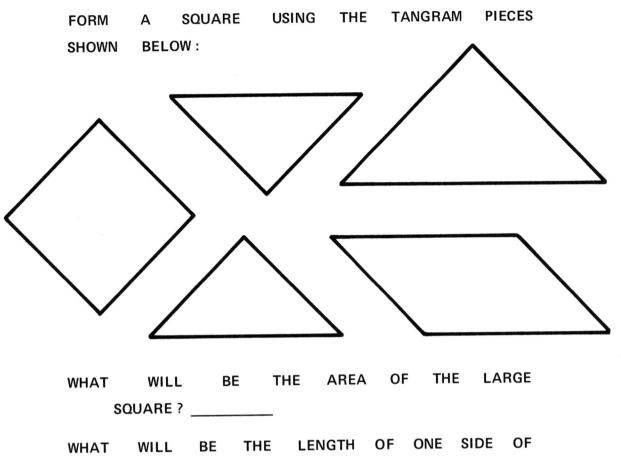

WHAT WILL BE THE AREA OF THE LARGE SQUARE? _____

WHAT WILL BE THE LENGTH OF ONE SIDE OF THE LARGE SQUARE? _____

USE THE PYTHAGOREAN THEOREM AND THE ANSWERS TO THE QUESTIONS ABOVE TO HELP SOLVE THIS PROBLEM.

A SQUARE CANNOT BE MADE USING THE SIX TANGRAM PIECES BELOW. USE YOUR KNOWLEDGE OF AREA AND THE PYTHAGOREAN THEOREM TO EXPLAIN WHY IT IS NOT POSSIBLE.

TANGRAM POLYGONS

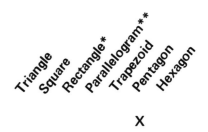

Pieces	Triangle	Square	Rectangle*	Parallelogram**	Trapezoid	Pentagon	Hexagon
1 1	X	X		X			
1 2					X		
1 3					X		
1 4					X		
3 4					X		
4 5					X		
5 5	X	X		X			
1 1 2	X		X	X	X		
1 1 3	X		X	X	X		
1 1 4	X	X	X	X	X		
1 1 5					X		
1 2 3					X		
1 2 4					X	X	
1 2 5						X	
1 3 4					X	X	
1 3 5					X		
1 4 5					X		
4 5 5					X	X	
1 1 2 3			X	X	X	X	X
1 1 2 4			X	X	X	X	X
1 1 2 5	X	X		X	X		
1 1 3 4			X	X	X	X	X
1 1 3 5	X	X		X	X		
1 1 4 5	X	X	X	X	X		
1 1 5 5						X	X
1 2 3 4					X	X	
1 2 3 5	X						
1 2 4 5	X						

Pieces	Triangle	Square	Rectangle*	Parallelogram**	Trapezoid	Pentagon	Hexagon
1 2 5 5						X	
1 3 4 5	X						X
1 3 5 5						X	
1 4 5 5						X	
1 1 2 3 4	X	X	X	X	X		X
1 1 2 3 5						X	X
1 1 2 4 5					X	X	X
1 1 2 5 5			X	X	X		
1 1 3 4 5					X	X	X
1 1 3 5 5			X	X	X		
1 1 4 5 5			X	X	X	X	X
1 2 3 4 5						X	
1 2 4 5 5						X	X
1 3 4 5 5						X	X
1 1 2 3 4 5			X	X	X		X
1 1 2 3 5 5						X	
1 1 2 4 5 5						X	X
1 1 3 4 5 5						X	X
1 2 3 4 5 5						X	
1 1 2 3 4 5 5	X	X	X	X	X	X	X

CODE: (Tangram Pieces)

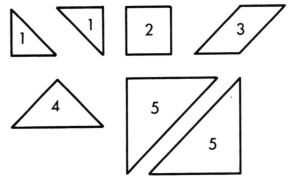

*   Rectangle that is not a square

**   Parallelogram that is not a rectangle

SUGGESTED ACTIVITIES

PART 3

1) How many different rectangular shapes can you make using one or more tangram pieces? How many different parallelograms? (Is a square a rectangle? Is a rectangle a parallelogram?)

2) Can you explain why a square cannot be made with any combination of six of the tangram pieces?

3) What interesting shapes can you make using a <u>double</u> set of tangrams (two regular sets combined)?

4) Have a tangram tournament.

SOLUTIONS

Page 7

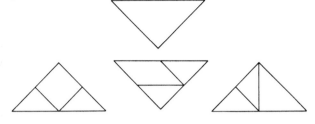

Page 8

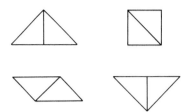

Page 11

5 Triangles
1 Square

Page 15

All tangram pieces have the same shape when turned over except the parallelogram.

Page 16

The parallelogram piece needs to be turned over in order to show two different solutions.

Page 17

A and B are the same size because each can be covered by the small triangle tangram.

C and D are the same size because each can be covered by the two small triangles.

Page 19

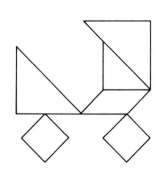

Page 20

The triangle and the square are the same size because each can be covered by the two small triangles.

The triangle and parallelogram are the same size because each can be covered by the two small triangles.

Page 21

Size

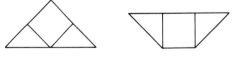

Page 22

Figure 1: One
Figure 2: Two
Figure 3: Four

Figures that have the same shape do not necessarily have the same size.

Page 23

Figures A and B are not the same shape, but they are the same size because each can be covered by the two small triangles and either the square, parallelogram or medium triangle.

Page 24

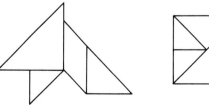

A is larger by one small tangram triangle.

TANGRAMATH ©1971 Creative Publications

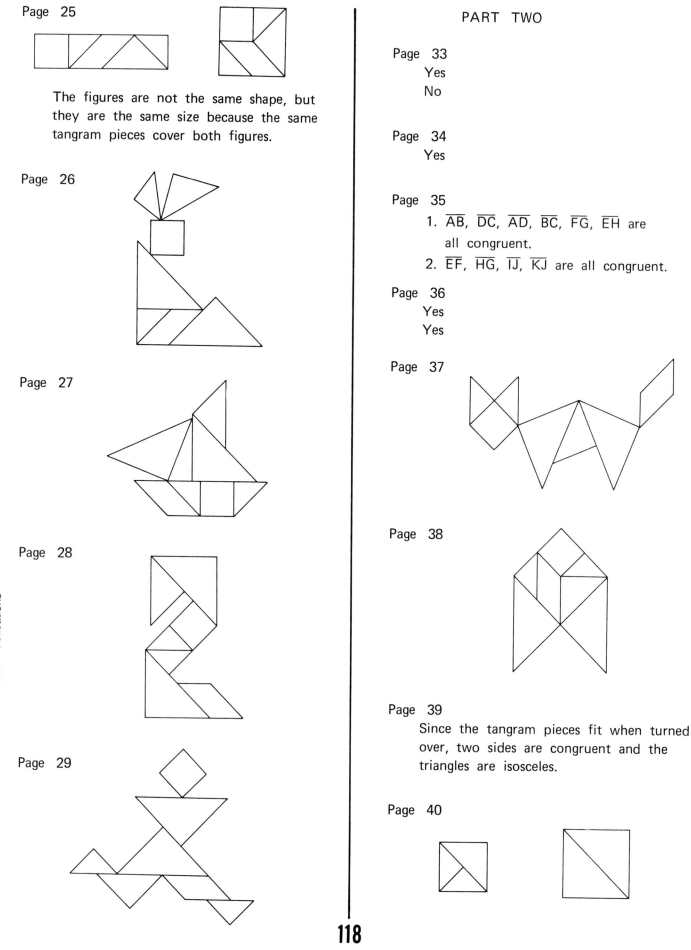

Page 25

The figures are not the same shape, but they are the same size because the same tangram pieces cover both figures.

Page 26

Page 27

Page 28

Page 29

PART TWO

Page 33
Yes
No

Page 34
Yes

Page 35
1. $\overline{AB}$, $\overline{DC}$, $\overline{AD}$, $\overline{BC}$, $\overline{FG}$, $\overline{EH}$ are all congruent.
2. $\overline{EF}$, $\overline{HG}$, $\overline{IJ}$, $\overline{KJ}$ are all congruent.

Page 36
Yes
Yes

Page 37

Page 38

Page 39
Since the tangram pieces fit when turned over, two sides are congruent and the triangles are isosceles.

Page 40

Page 41
　　Yes
　　Yes

Page 42

Page 43

Page 44

Page 45
　　Yes
　　Yes
　　Yes

Page 46

Page 47

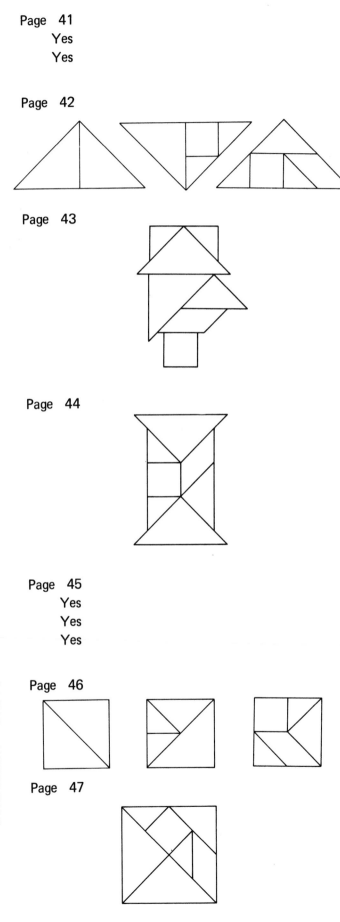

Page 48

Page 49

Page 50

Page 52

Page 53

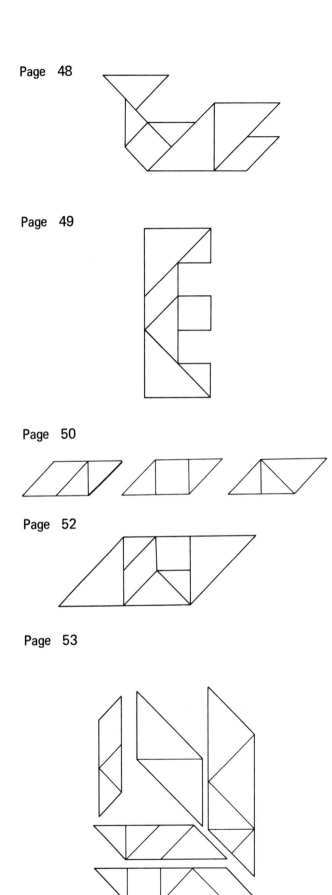

Page 55

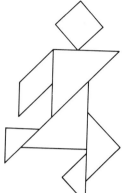

Page 56

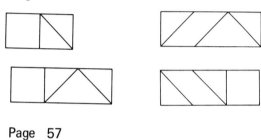

Page 57
   Yes
   Yes
   Yes

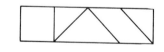

Page 58

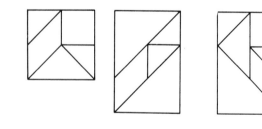

Page 59

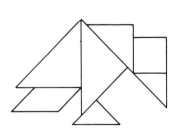

PART THREE

Page 62
   A = 1   D = 2
   B = 2   E = 4
   C = 2

Page 63
   Area is 16

Page 64

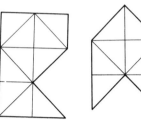

   Area is 10   Area is 8

Page 65

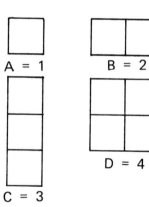

Page 66
   Two small tangram triangles cover each figure.

   No.   Yes.   No.

Page 67
   A = 1   B = 1

Page 68
   A = 2   C = 1
   B = 1   D = 2

TANGRAMATH ©1971 Creative Publications

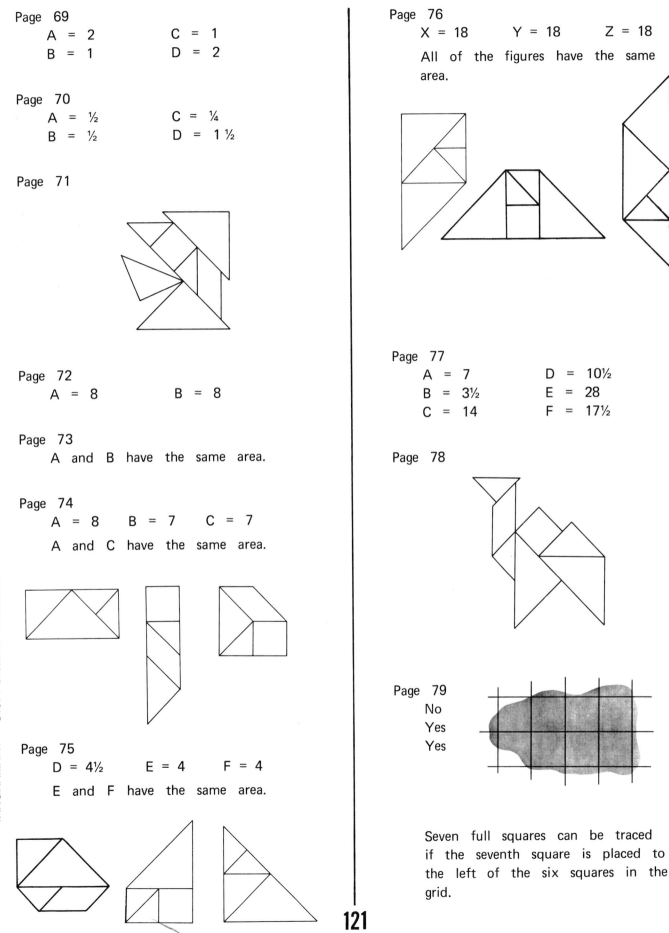

Page 69
A = 2　　　　C = 1
B = 1　　　　D = 2

Page 70
A = ½　　　　C = ¼
B = ½　　　　D = 1 ½

Page 71

Page 72
A = 8　　　　　　B = 8

Page 73
A and B have the same area.

Page 74
A = 8　　B = 7　　C = 7
A and C have the same area.

Page 75
D = 4½　　　E = 4　　　F = 4
E and F have the same area.

Page 76
X = 18　　　Y = 18　　　Z = 18
All of the figures have the same area.

Page 77
A = 7　　　　D = 10½
B = 3½　　　E = 28
C = 14　　　F = 17½

Page 78

Page 79
No
Yes
Yes

Seven full squares can be traced if the seventh square is placed to the left of the six squares in the grid.

TANGRAMATH

121

Page 80
Squares would be better.

The area of the sheet is about 41 tangram squares.

The small triangle tangram would be easier to use for measuring.

Page 81
The area is <u>one</u> square unit.

Page 82
D = 2 square units
E = 3 square units
F = 6 square units

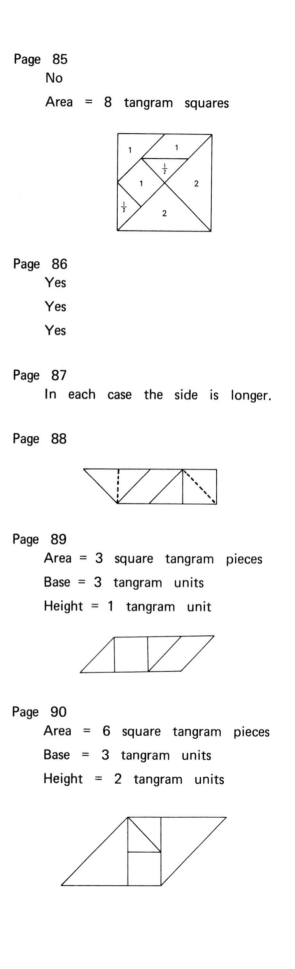

Page 83
B = 2 square units
C — Length: 3
Width: 1
Area: 3 x 1 = 3 sq. units

Page 84
Area = 6 square tangram pieces
Length = 3
Width = 2

Page 85
No
Area = 8 tangram squares

Page 86
Yes
Yes
Yes

Page 87
In each case the side is longer.

Page 88

Page 89
Area = 3 square tangram pieces
Base = 3 tangram units
Height = 1 tangram unit

Page 90
Area = 6 square tangram pieces
Base = 3 tangram units
Height = 2 tangram units

Page 91

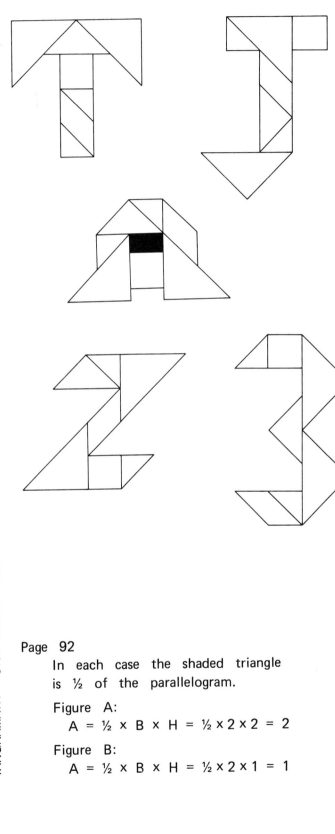

Page 92

In each case the shaded triangle is ½ of the parallelogram.

Figure A:
$A = ½ \times B \times H = ½ \times 2 \times 2 = 2$

Figure B:
$A = ½ \times B \times H = ½ \times 2 \times 1 = 1$

Page 93

Area = 4 square tangram pieces
Base = 4 tangram units
Height = 2 tangram units

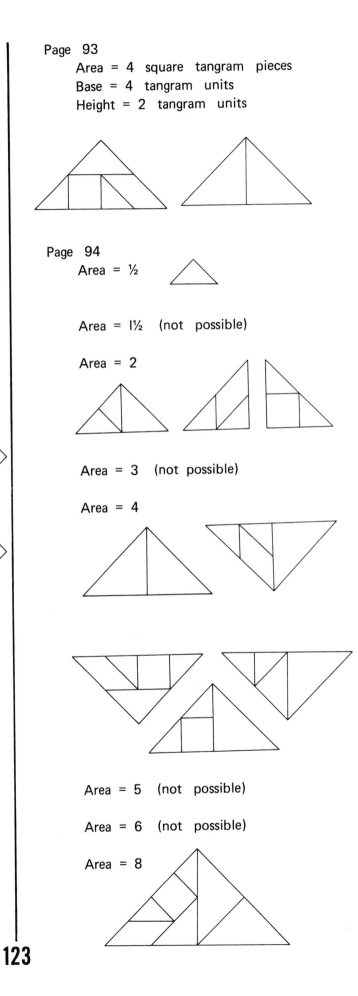

Page 94

Area = ½

Area = 1½ (not possible)

Area = 2

Area = 3 (not possible)

Area = 4

Area = 5 (not possible)

Area = 6 (not possible)

Area = 8

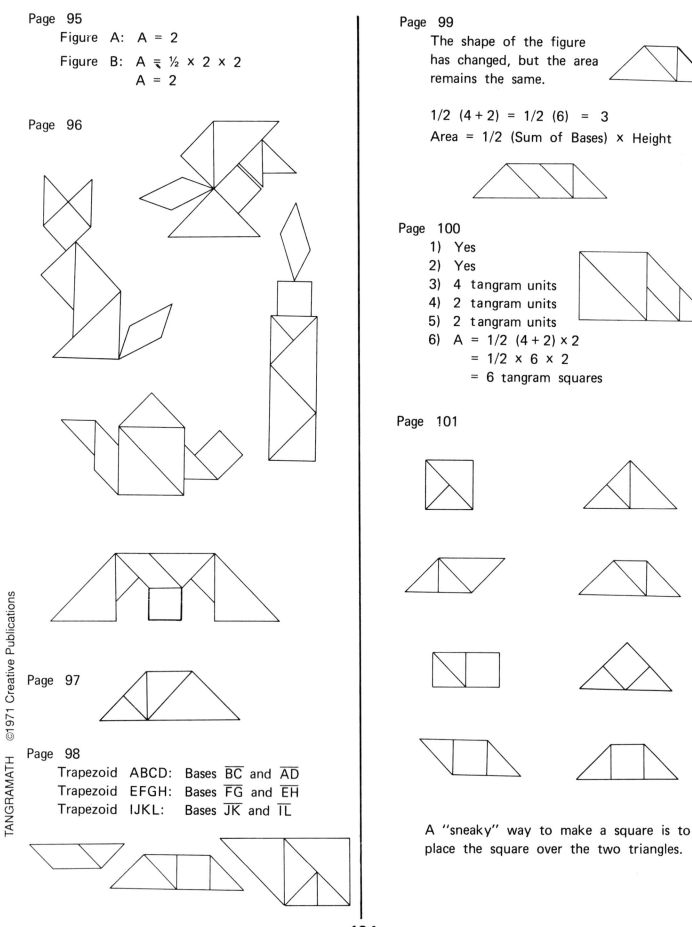

Page 95

Figure A: A = 2

Figure B: A = ½ × 2 × 2

A = 2

Page 96

Page 97

Page 98

Trapezoid ABCD: Bases $\overline{BC}$ and $\overline{AD}$

Trapezoid EFGH: Bases $\overline{FG}$ and $\overline{EH}$

Trapezoid IJKL: Bases $\overline{JK}$ and $\overline{IL}$

Page 99

The shape of the figure has changed, but the area remains the same.

1/2 (4 + 2) = 1/2 (6) = 3

Area = 1/2 (Sum of Bases) × Height

Page 100

1) Yes

2) Yes

3) 4 tangram units

4) 2 tangram units

5) 2 tangram units

6) A = 1/2 (4 + 2) × 2

= 1/2 × 6 × 2

= 6 tangram squares

Page 101

A "sneaky" way to make a square is to place the square over the two triangles.

TANGRAMATH ©1971 Creative Publications

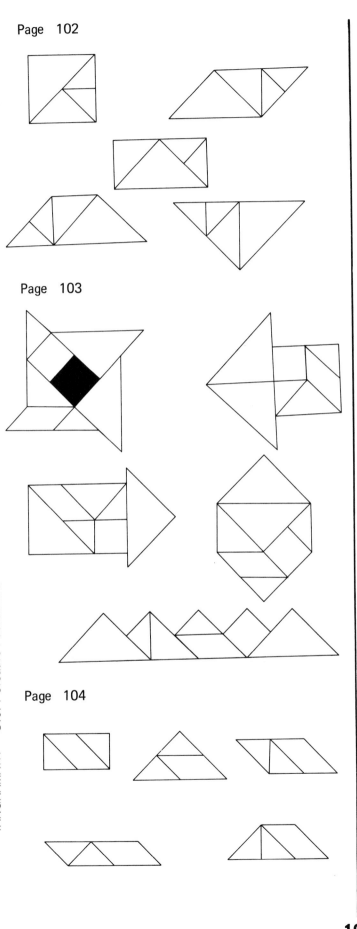

Page 102

Page 103

Page 104

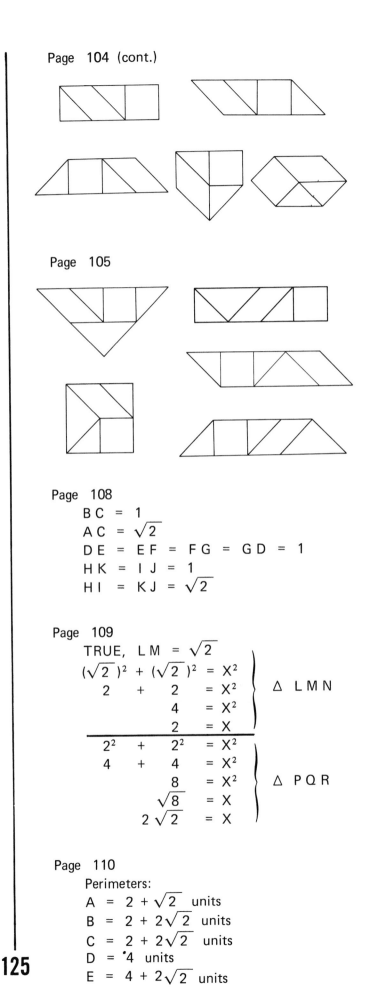

Page 105

Page 108
$$B C = 1$$
$$A C = \sqrt{2}$$
$$D E = E F = F G = G D = 1$$
$$H K = I J = 1$$
$$H I = K J = \sqrt{2}$$

Page 109
TRUE, $L M = \sqrt{2}$

$$\left.\begin{array}{rcl}(\sqrt{2})^2 + (\sqrt{2})^2 &=& X^2 \\ 2 + 2 &=& X^2 \\ 4 &=& X^2 \\ 2 &=& X\end{array}\right\} \triangle LMN$$

$$\left.\begin{array}{rcl}2^2 + 2^2 &=& X^2 \\ 4 + 4 &=& X^2 \\ 8 &=& X^2 \\ \sqrt{8} &=& X \\ 2\sqrt{2} &=& X\end{array}\right\} \triangle PQR$$

Page 110
Perimeters:
$A = 2 + \sqrt{2}$ units
$B = 2 + 2\sqrt{2}$ units
$C = 2 + 2\sqrt{2}$ units
$D = $ ˙4 units
$E = 4 + 2\sqrt{2}$ units

125

Page 110 (cont.)

Areas:

A = 1/2 square unit

B = 1 square unit

C = 1 square unit

D = 1 square unit

E = 2 square units

Page 111

m $(\overline{AB})$ = 2

m $(\overline{BC})$ = 2

m $(\overline{DC})$ = $\sqrt{2}$

m $(\overline{AD})$ = $\sqrt{2}$

Area of ABCD is 3 square units.

m $(\overline{EF})$ = $3\sqrt{2}$

m $(\overline{FG})$ = $\sqrt{2}$

m $(\overline{GH})$ = $2\sqrt{2}$

m $(\overline{HE})$ = 2

Area of EFGH is 5 square units.

Page 113

Area = 4 square units

Length = 2 units

You can form the side of the square from the possibilities of 1, $\sqrt{2}$, 2.

Page 114

Area would be 6 square units.

Length of one side would be $\sqrt{6}$ units.

You cannot form $\sqrt{6}$ from combinations of 1, $\sqrt{2}$, 2, $2\sqrt{2}$.